Iditarod Fact Book

Iditarod Fact Book

A Complete Guide to the Last Great Race®

Edited by Sue Mattson
Photographs by Jeff Schultz
Illustrations by Jon Van Zyle
Research by Andrea Bachhuber

EPICENTER PRESS
Alaska Book Adventures

EPICENTER PRESS is a regional press founded in Alaska whose interests include but are not limited to the arts, history, environment, and diverse cultures and lifestyles of the North Pacific and high latitudes. We seek both the traditional and innovative in publishing high-quality non-fiction tradebooks, contemporary art and photography giftbooks, and destination travel guides emphasizing Alaska, Washington, Oregon, and California.

The Iditarod Committee© holds registered trademarks for the following terms and languages: Iditarod®, Iditarod Trail Committee®, Iditarod Trail Alaska®, Alaska where men are men and women win the Iditarod®, The Last Great Race®, 1,049 miles®, Anchorage to Nome®, and Mushing the Iditarod Trail®.

Publisher: Kent Sturgis
Researcher: Andrea Bachhuber
Cover and Inside Design: Sue Mattson
Map: Marge Mueller, Gray Mouse Graphics
Photographs: © 2001 Jeff Schultz/Alaskastock except as noted
Proofreader: Sherrill Carlson
Printer: Transcontinental Printing
Text © 2001 Epicenter Press
Cover illustration © 2000 Jon VanZyle

Library of Congress Catalog Card Number: 00 136167

To order IDITAROD FACT BOOK mail $12.95 plus $4.95 for shipping (Washington residents add $1.14 sales tax) to Epicenter Press, Box 82368, Kenmore, WA 98028; visit our website, www.EpicenterPress.com; or call 800-950-6663.

Booksellers: Retail discounts are offered from our trade distributor, Graphic Arts Center Publishing™, Box 10306, Portland, OR 97210.

First Edition
First printing February 2001
10 9 8 7 6 5 4 3 2 1
PRINTED IN CANADA

Contents

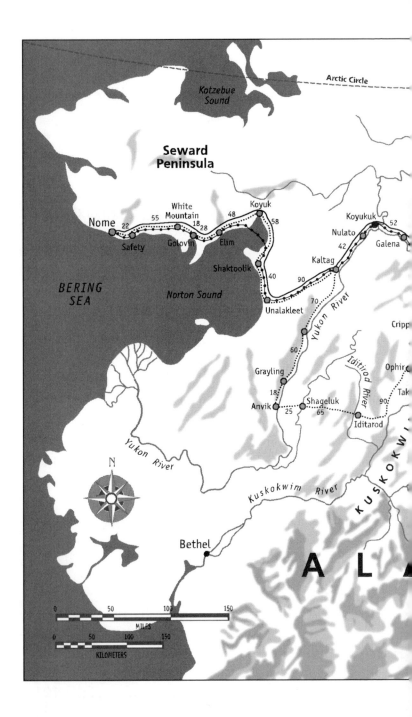

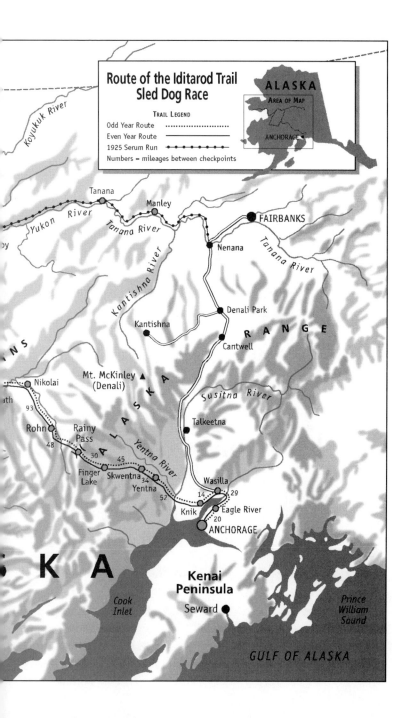

Route of the Iditarod Trail Sled Dog Race

TRAIL LEGEND

Odd Year Route ··············
Even Year Route ─────
1925 Serum Run ●─●─●─●
Numbers = mileages between checkpoints

ALASKA
AREA OF MAP
ANCHORAGE

Koyukuk River

Tanana

Manley

FAIRBANKS

Yukon River

Tanana River

Nenana

Tanana River

Kantishna River

Denali Park

Kantishna

RANGE

Cantwell

Nikolai

93

Mt. McKinley ▲
(Denali)

Susitna River

Rohn

48

Rainy
Pass

ALASKA

Yentna River

Talkeetna

30

45

Finger
Lake

Skwentna

34

Yentna

52

Wasilla

14

29

Knik

Eagle River

20

ANCHORAGE

S K A

Kenai
Peninsula

Cook
Inlet

Seward

Prince
William
Sound

GULF OF ALASKA

The Race

BIB NUMBER ONE

The Iditarod's bib number one traditionally was reserved to honor Leonhard Seppala, the most famous of the mushers who transported lifesaving diphtheria serum in the historic Nenana-to-Nome run of 1925. From 1973 to 1980, Seppala was named as honorary musher.

In 1980, "Wild Bill" Shannon was chosen jointly with Seppala. Each year since then, the Iditarod Trail Committee has named as honorary mushers one or more individuals who have made a significant contribution to the sport, even if they are not mushers. Bib number one is reserved for them.

See also: HONORARY MUSHERS

CLOSEST FINISH

In 1978, Dick Mackey took first place in a stunning one-second finish when his lead dog crossed the finish line a nose ahead of Rick Swenson's leader. Mackey finished in 14 days, 18 hours, 52 minutes, and 24 seconds. The one-second difference cost Swenson $4,000 in prize money. Mackey won $12,000; Swenson $8,000.

Photo, Page 10

CORRALLING RULE

Before this rule was adopted in 1992, mushers were allowed to stay in villagers' homes when they stopped at checkpoints. The corralling rule dictates that all mushers rest in the same sleeping area so officials can be assured that no musher receives illegal assistance, and veterinarians don't have to traipse all over the villages looking for teams they're assigned to check.

Iditarod Country, *Epicenter Press*

CHAMPIONS, 1973-2000

Year	Musher	Hometown	D/H/M/S
1973	Dick Wilmarth	Red Devil, AK	20:00:49:4
1974	Carl Huntington	Galena, AK	20:15:02:0
1975	Emmitt Peters	Ruby, AK	14:14:43:4
1976	Gerald Riley	Nenana, AK	18:22:58:1
1977	Rick Swenson	Manley, AK	16:16:27:1
1978	Dick Mackey	Wasilla, AK	14:18:52:2
1979	Rick Swenson	Manley, AK	15:10:37:4
1980	Joe May	Trapper Ck., AK	14:07:11:5
1981	Rick Swenson	Manley, AK	12:08:45:0
1982	Rick Swenson	Manley, AK	16:04:40:1
1983	Rick Mackey	Wasilla, AK	12:14:10:4
1984	Dean Osmar	Clam Gulch, AK	12:15:07:3
1985	Libby Riddles	Teller, AK	18:00:20:1
1986	Susan Butcher	Manley, AK	11:15:06:0
1987	Susan Butcher	Manley, AK	11:02:05:1
1988	Susan Butcher	Manley, AK	11:11:41:4
1989	Joe Runyan	Nenana, AK	11:05:24:3
1990	Susan Butcher	Manley, AK	11:01:53:2
1991	Rick Swenson	Two Rivers, AK	12:16:34:3
1992	Martin Buser	Big Lake, AK	10:19:17:0
1993	Jeff King	Denali, AK	10:15:38:1
1994	Martin Buser	Big Lake, AK	10:13:02:3
1995	Doug Swingley	Simms, MT	09:02:42:1
1996	Jeff King	Denali, AK	09:05:43:1
1997	Martin Buser	Big Lake, AK	09:08:30:4
1998	Jeff King	Denali, AK	09:05:52:2
1999	Doug Swingley	Lincoln, MT	09:14:31:0
2000	Doug Swingley	Lincoln, MT	09:00:58:0

© Rob Stapleton/Alaskastock

Dick Mackey beat Rick Swenson by one second in 1978—the closest finish ever in the Iditarod.

DISTANCE

No one knows the true distance for sure, because the trail weaves through the natural terrain and its routing is often affected by the weather. Race officials use 1,049 as the symbolic distance (Alaska was the forty-ninth state to be admitted to the union) but most estimates suggest the trail is at least 1,100 miles long.

ENTRY FEE

The entry fee, at least $1,750 in recent years, includes Iditarod and P.R.I.D.E. membership dues. The fee may be paid beginning in late June and must be paid no later than December 1.

Iditarod Policies, 2001

FINANCES

Sled dog racing is an expensive sport. Minimum expense for a musher to enter a team in the Iditarod is estimated at $15,000, but this figure can reach $100,000 for a truly competitive team.

Many dogs in the kennel are worth $2,000 or more, and this figure increases to more than $8,000 for a fully trained lead dog.

Race expenses include dog food, the entry fees, harnesses, booties, and airfare for a long-distance race. Sleds, clothing, equipment that can be reused year after year also are expensive. Mushers living in rural areas pay significantly more money for the upkeep of their kennels, as everything must be flown in or out, including themselves and their dogs for the beginning of the race.

FINISHERS
See: APPENDIX III

FIRST PRIZE, 1973-2001

Year	Amount	Year	Amount
1973	$12,000	1988	$30,000
1974	$12,000	1989	$50,000
1975	$15,000	1990	$50,000
1976	$7,200	1991	$50,000
1977	$9,600	1992	$51,600
1978	$12,000	1993	$50,000
1979	$12,000	1994	$50,000
1980	$12,000	1995	$52,500
1981	$24,000	1996	$50,000
1982	$24,000	1997	$50,000
1983	$24,000	1998	$51,000
1984	$24,000	1999	$60,000
1985	$50,000	2000	$60,000
1986	$50,000	2001	$62,857
1987	$50,000		

HAZARDS

Mushing 1,100 miles across Alaska's wilderness is not without hazards. Mushers may encounter wild animals, including moose, buffalo, caribou, and wolves. Fallen trees may block the trail, and in the Rainy Pass area, avalanches are not uncommon. Overflow or thin ice may hide frigid water on the trail. Heavy snows, white-out conditions, and even blizzards may hamper visibility. Severe cold weather may bring frostbite and hypothermia; strong winds are another hazard. Dogs can run away, or lose the trail. Hard-driving mushers risk falling asleep and have hallucinations from lack of sleep. Falling off the sled can happen at any time.

HISTORY OF THE RACE

Mush dog teams a thousand miles across the wilderness? In 1973, many thought it couldn't be done. But a core of believers, led by the man who became known as the Father of Iditarod, thought it could and set out to prove it.

The idea of a race along the historic Iditarod Trail had been talked about for years. In 1967, the 100th anniversary of Alaska's purchase from Russia, a Wasilla woman named Dorothy G. Page promoted the idea of holding a sled dog race as part of the celebration. The race was held on a section of the old Iditarod Trail for a distance of 28 miles. Could dogs race more than a thousand miles along that trail from Anchorage all the way to Nome? The one true believer was Joe Redington Sr., a small, leathery-faced sourdough who came to Alaska from Oklahoma, founded a kennel in Knik, and devoted much of his life to mushing.

By 1973, Redington was ready. Originally, he proposed a race from Anchorage to Iditarod, the mining ghost town some 500 miles down the trail. Dick Mackey, an Anchorage sprint musher, was enthused listening to Redington and saw possibilities in a long-distance event. "No one's heard of Iditarod. Why don't you run to Nome?" Done!

Redington worked with Tom Johnson and Gleo Huyck to organize the race, but when Redington guaranteed a purse of $50,000, the mushing community was astounded. At the time, according to Howard Farley, also an organizer, there wasn't $50,000 in prize money offered for all the dog races in the world combined. But the promised purse became reality when old World War

II Eskimo Scouts leader Col. "Muktuk" Marston donated $10,000 and the Bank of the North approved the cosigning of a $30,000 loan for Redington by local businessman Bruce Kendall. Redington put up his Knik home as collateral, and the frantic fund-raising effort kept him from entering the race he created.

When the first Saturday in March arrived in 1973, thirty-six dog teams lined up at the Anchorage starting line at the Tudor Track sprint complex. As they set out on the trail, the issue was whether anyone would finish. Yet a feeling of excitement pervaded the mushers, a feeling of being in on the ground floor of something new, perhaps a once-in-a-lifetime race.

At the first Iditarod pre-race banquet, George Attla of North Pole, the ten-time world sprint mushing champion, announced he had conferred with Athabascan elders for an estimate of how long it should take the dogs to run to Nome. The race, proclaimed Attla, would take ten days. Attla and the elders were right—but it took most of two decades for the race to evolve into a ten-day event. The first ten-day Iditarod winning time was recorded in 1992, when Martin Buser of Big Lake notched his first victory. The mushers of 1973 truly headed off into the unknown. Twenty days and 49 minutes later, Dick Wilmarth crossed the finish line in Nome, the winner of the debut Iditarod. Bobby Vent was second, Dan Seavey third, and Attla fourth.

One characteristic emerging in the first Iditarod has persisted. The race is for everybody, the fast and the slow. For many, the most coveted prize of all is earning an Iditarod finisher's belt buckle.

Of the thirty-six teams that started the 1973 race,

twenty-two completed the run to Nome. John Schulz finished in 32 days, 5 hours, nearly two weeks behind Wilmarth. Schulz was the first recipient of a special prize that is still awarded for last place—the Red Lantern (although his was blue as no one could find a red one).

At the first finishers' banquet in Nome, Redington asked if the race should be run again the next year. A mighty roar went up. The Iditarod was established.

Iditarod Silver, *Epicenter Press*

IDITA-RIDER PROGRAM

A fund-raiser in which fans bid for the privilege of riding in a musher's sled during the first stretch of the race from Anchorage to the power station where Tudor and Muldoon roads meet. Proceeds pay up to $1,049 to each musher finishing from thirty-first place to last place.

Bidding is open from the first Monday in November through the last Friday in January, and then bidders may participate in live teleconference bidding that determines the winners.

IDITAROD, definition

One definition says "Iditarod" is a Shageluk Indian word meaning *clear water,* used in the name of the Iditarod River. Another source claims that it's an Ingalik Indian word, "Haiditarod," meaning *distant place.* Yet another version comes from Professor James Kari of the University of Alaska Native Language Center: "The name 'Iditarod' came from an Ingalik and Holikachuk word, 'hidedhod,' for the Iditarod River. This name means *distant* or *distant place*."

Iditarod Silver, *Epicenter Press*

ITC

Acronym for Iditarod Trail Committee®.

JUNIOR IDITAROD®

The Junior Iditarod race begins on the last Saturday of February, providing an opportunity for mushers ages 14 through 17 to race along a portion of the Iditarod Trail.

The Junior Iditarod was first run in 1977, organized by Karl Clauson, Kenny Pugh, Clarence Shockley, and Eric Beeman.

The young mushers follow the Iditarod Trail for about 60 miles, starting in Wasilla, overnighting at the Yentna Station Roadhouse, and then returning to Wasilla. The junior drivers stay with their dogs during the overnight stop, caring for them just as the adult mushers do during the Iditarod.

Many Junior Iditarod mushers have gone on to compete in the Iditarod, including Tim Osmar, three-time winner of the Junior Iditarod; Andy Willis, a three-time junior finisher; Kimarie Hansen, also a three-time junior finisher; as well as Karl Clauson, Rome Gilman, Clarence Shockley, Jason and Laird Barron, Aaron Burmeister, Simon Kineen, and Cim and Ramey Smyth.

KILLING OF GAME ANIMALS

"In the event that an edible big game animal, i.e., moose, caribou, buffalo, is killed in defense of life or property, the musher must gut the animal and report the incident to a race official at the next checkpoint. Following teams must help gut the animal when possible. No teams may pass until the animal has been gutted and the musher killing the animal has proceeded.

Any other animal killed in defense of life or property must be reported to a race official, but need not be gutted."

Iditarod Rules, 2001

MANDATORY STOPS

Three mandatory stops are required. For the 2001 race, these stops were specified in the race rules as:

"Twenty-Four Hour Stop: A musher must take one mandatory twenty-four (24) hour stop during the race. The twenty-four (24) hour stop may be taken at the musher's option at a time most beneficial to the dogs. The checker must be notified by the musher that he/she is taking his/her twenty-four (24) hour stop. Time begins upon notification. The starting differential will be adjusted during each team's twenty-four (24) hour stop. It is the musher's responsibility to remain for the entire twenty-four (24) hour period plus starting differential. The ITC will give each musher the required time information prior to leaving the starting line.

"Eight Hour Mandatory Stops: In addition to the mandatory twenty-four (24) hour stop, a musher must take one eight (8) hour stop on the Yukon and one eight (8) hour stop at White Mountain.

"None of the three (3) mandatory stops may be combined."

MOOSE

Moose may be encountered anywhere along the Iditarod Trail. Alaska's largest mammal, the bulls may weigh 1,600 pounds and the cows 1,300. Only bulls carry antlers, which are shed each fall and then regrown. Although

moose generally are not aggressive, they are unpredictable, and cows with calves are fiercely protective. In deep snow, they may seek out the easier going of hard-packed trails and may be reluctant to give way to oncoming dog teams.

Inevitably, Iditarod mushers have had encounters with moose. In 1985, a moose attacked Susan Butcher's team, killing two of her dogs and injuring thirteen, forcing her to scratch from the race. Many fans believe Butcher would have won the race that year if not for the attack.

In 1980, Jerry Austin and Dick Mackey killed a moose that attacked their teams. They were charged with wasting the meat, but the charges were dropped.

In 1995, Austin stopped a charging moose with an explosive shot fired from a flare pistol.

NAVIGATION

"Mushers are restricted to the use of traditional forms of navigation. This includes time, distance as known or measured on a map, speed as is computed with simple arithmetic and direction as indicated by magnetic compass. Electronic or mechanical devices that measure speed and direction are prohibited, i.e. Loran, night vision goggles and GPS."

Iditarod Rules, 2001

PURSE

For the 2001 race, the purse, or total prize money to be paid to winners, was set at $550,000, paid out as follows:

1st Place	$62,857	16th Place	12,571
2nd Place	55,000	17th Place	12,048
3rd Place	47,143	18th Place	11,262
4th Place	39,286	19th Place	10,738
5th Place	35,619	20th Place	9,952
6th Place	32,476	21st Place	8,381
7th Place	29,857	22nd Place	7,333
8th Place	27,238	23rd Place	6,286
9th Place	24,619	24th Place	4,190
10th Place	22,000	25th Place	3,667
11th Place	19,381	26th Place	2,619
12th Place	17,286	27th Place	2,095
13th Place	14,667	28th Place	1,833
14th Place	13,619	29th Place	1,571
15th Place	13,095	30th Place	1,310

Iditarod Policies, 2001

RACE CATEGORIES

Sprint races vary in length and usually are run in heats over two or three days. There are hundreds of sprint races, in Alaska and elsewhere around the world. Top sprint races in Alaska are the Fur Rondezvous World Championship in Anchorage in February, and the Open North American Championship in Fairbanks, in March.

Middle distance races are usually more than 100 miles, and as much as 300 to 500 miles. There are a growing number of these races; an example is the Kuskokwim 300 in Bethel, Alaska, in mid-January.

Long distance or endurance races cover more than 500 miles, and include the Iditarod Trail Sled Dog Race from Anchorage to Nome each March, and the Yukon Quest between Fairbanks, Alaska, and Whitehorse, British Columbia, Canada, each February.

RACE POLICIES

See: APPENDIX I

RACE RULES

See: APPENDIX II

RED LANTERN

One of the great symbols of the Iditarod Trail Sled Dog Race is the Red Lantern, the award for finishing last. The Red Lantern has been presented to the last finisher in every Iditarod, beginning with John Schulz in 1973, the

© Jeff Schultz/Alaskastock

slowest of the slow, who took more than 32 days to complete route. Why a red lantern? It's more or less a statement that those who passed that way before will leave a light burning for you.

Iditarod Silver, *Epicenter Press*

© Jeff Schultz/Alaskastock

Timing begins when mushers leave the restart line in Wasilla, as does DeeDee Jonrowe in 2000.

RESTART

After the teams mush from Anchorage to Eagle River on Saturday, they are trucked to Wasilla, avoiding open water on the Knik River and the often snowless Palmer Flats. At Wasilla on Sunday, the race is restarted, and the official clock begins running. Teams leave the Wasilla starting line at two-minute intervals, and the time difference is adjusted later during the 24-hour mandatory stop. No time is kept between Anchorage and Eagle River.

REST STOPS

When the mushers halt their teams for a rest at checkpoint or along the trail, hrnesses are removed and dogs are usually secured only by their necklines. They are rubbed down and their ankles and shoulders are sweat-wrapped. Then their booties are removed and each paw is checked and treated for splits and cracks.

Quickly, they fall asleep as their driver locates his or her supply sacks and fuel. He then sets up the stove and fetches water. At checkpoints, hot water is often provided, but if the rest stop comes on the trail, the musher may have to heat it. While waiting, the musher begins to chop up frozen blocks of meat to add to the water. Commercial dry food, fat, and supplements are stirred in, and then cool water is mixed in until the meal is of an acceptable temperature for the hungry team.

Some mushers choose to feed their leaders first and then work their way down the team, always patting and sweet talking each dog while feeding it.

Finally, the driver disposes of trash, returns unused fuel, eats his own meal, chats with his fellow competitors, consults with a vet, and finally falls into a brief catnap before returning to the trail. Top long-distance runners get approximately two hours of sleep per day, averaging out to a 40 minute nap at each rest stop.

SCRATCH

To drop out of the race after it has begun.

SERUM RUN

The year was 1925, the month was January—the depths of winter—and the town was Nome. The children of the village had been exposed to diphtheria and needed lifesaving antitoxin serum. Mushers responded, and a tale of heroism ensued.

The story began when Dr. Curtis Welch diagnosed the diphtheria outbreak. Diphtheria is a serious contagious bacterial disease marked by high fever, weakness, and the formation in the throat and other air passages of false membranes that cause difficulty in breathing. In children in particular, it can be fatal.

Dr. Welch sent telegrams to Fairbanks, Anchorage, Seward, and Juneau asking for help. The only serum available was in Anchorage at the Alaska Railroad Hospital, where Dr. J.B. Beeson had 300,000 units. But Anchorage to Nome is more than 1,000 miles, and no planes were available to make the flight. Time was of the essence.

Governor Scott C. Bone decided the speediest and most reliable way to get the serum to Nome was via dog sled. He called on the Northern Commercial Company, the largest organization in the Yukon River area, to arrange for relay teams.

The serum was packed up in Anchorage in a cylinder. Dr. Beeson wrapped it in a quilt for insulation, then it was tied up in canvas for protection. The first part of the journey was by train from Anchorage to Nenana. The train arrived in Nenana on Tuesday, January 27, 1925, at 11:00 P.M. Conductor Frank Knight gave the bundle to the first of twenty mushers, William "Wild Bill" Shannon, who took it on the first leg of the 674 miles to Nome.

When Leonhard Seppala's turn approached, he left Nome, intending to rest at Nulato and return with the serum. But before he reached Nulato, he met Myles Gonangnan at Shaktoolik. Seppala took the serum from Gonangnan, and without stopping to rest, turned around and headed back to Nome.

He crossed the frozen Norton Sound with temperatures hovering at 30 degrees below zero. The weather was brutal, with a merciless gale blowing and the trail hard to follow in the frozen north's winter darkness, even with his lead dog Togo at the head of the team. Still, he made it to Golovin, 91 miles down the trail, after travelling a total of 260 miles.

Finally, after the serum was carried by 19 other mushers, Gunner Kaasen drove his tired dog team—led by another of Seppala's lead dogs, Balto—down an almost deserted First Avenue on February 2, 1925. The serum had reached the town in an epic run lasting 127 $1/_2$ hours.

Today's Iditarod Trail Sled Dog Race follows some of the same route used by those mushers more than seventy-five years ago.

Iditarod Trail Committee website: www.Iditarod.com

SLOGAN

The Iditarod's slogan, "The Last Great Race on Earth®," originated with Ian Wooldridge, a sports reporter for the *London Daily Mail,* who followed the race in 1978 and called it "the Last Great Race on Earth." The phrase is now a registered trademark held by the Iditarod Trail Committee.

SPECIAL AWARDS

Each year special awards are given to mushers in the Iditarod. In 2000, the following awards were given:

Lolly Medley Golden Harness Award: Handmade harness recognizing the outstanding lead dog of the race. Originally presented each year by harness maker Lolly Medley, one of two women to run the second Iditarod in 1974. She died in 1997. The award is now given in her memory by the city of Nome.

Alaska Airlines Leonhard Seppala Humanitarian Award: To the musher in the top twenty who has best demonstrated outstanding care of his or her team through the race while remaining competitive. Selected by veterinary staff and race officials. Lead crystal cup on an illuminated wooden base; transportation back to Anchorage for musher and dogs; two round-trip tickets to anywhere Alaska Airlines flies.

Rookie of the Year: To the top-placing man or woman racing his or her first Iditarod. Trophy and $1,500 prize presented by Jerry and Clara Austin.

Sportsmanship Award: Selected by mushers; winner receives an engraved crystal award.

Most Improved Musher: Recognizes the most improved musher with an engraved crystal award.

Providence Health System Most Inspirational Musher Award: Official finishers decide who among themselves was most inspirational on the trail. Winner receives a framed Charles Gauss painting.

GCI Dorothy G. Page Halfway Award: Presented at Iditarod, the halfway checkpoint in odd years when the race follows the southern route and at Cripple in even years when the race follows the northern route. Winners receive a trophy and $3,000 in gold. A perpetual trophy made of Alaskan birch and marble, featuring a photograph of the late Dorothy G. Page, remains year-round at Iditarod headquarters in Wasilla.

National Bank of Alaska's Gold Coast Award: A trophy and $2,500 in gold nuggets goes to the first musher to arrive in Unalakleet, on the coast. A perpetual trophy commemorating the award remains year round at the Iditarod headquarters in Wasilla.

Regal Alaskan's First Musher to the Yukon Award: A seven-course gourmet meal prepared by the executive chef of the Regal Alaskan Hotel awaits the first musher to the Yukon River. The winner also receives $3,500 in $1 bills.

Fastest Time from Safety to Nome: A long-standing award presented by the Nome Kennel Club, $500 goes to the musher who finishes in the top twenty and has the fastest time from Safety to Nome.

The Alaska Dodge Dealers Official Truck Award: Keys to a fully loaded Dodge truck are handed to the winner of the Iditarod Trail Sled Dog race at the finish line in Nome.

Cabela's Outfitter Award: $1,000 gift certificate is awarded to a musher selected in a random drawing.

Golden Stethoscope Award: Presented by the Iditarod Official Finishers Club to a veterinarian on the trail.

The National Bank of Alaska Red Lantern Award: The last musher across the finish line is presented with a Red Lantern and earns a place in Iditarod history.

Pen Air Spirit of Alaska Award: A beautiful framed spirit mask presented to the first musher into McGrath.

SPONSORS

Sponsors are critical to the survival of dog mushing and sled dog racing. Corporations, businesses, and individuals sponsor individual mushers as well as particular races.

Maintaining a kennel of racing dogs is no small commitment, not least of which is financial. Sponsors make it possible for many mushers and racers to continue.

Recent sponsors of the Iditarod have included:

Presenting Sponsors: Alaska Dodge Dealers, Cabela's, GCI, National Bank of Alaska.

Major Sponsors: Alaska Airlines, Alaska's SuperStation, Fred Meyer Stores, Globalstar USA, Pen Air, Providence Alaska Medical Center, Regal Alaskan Hotel.

Supporting Sponsors: Anchorage Daily News, Anchorage 5th Avenue Mall, Chevron, City of Nome, Municipality of Anchorage, Northern Air Cargo, True Value Hardware, Yupo Corporation.

Sponsors: Alaska Newspapers, Alaska Serigraphics, Alaska Sightseeing/Cruise West, Alcan Signs, Budget Feed/Alaska Grown Dog Food, Burger King, City of Wasilla, COMTEC Business Systems, Coors Brewing

Company, Cottonwood Creek Mall, Crowley Marine Services, EXXON Company USA, Fort Dodge Animal Health, Hawaiian Vacations, Holland America Lines Westours, Interbake Foods, Nome Kennel Club, North Mail, Professional Colorgraphics, Seagrams Crown Royal, Sears, Tilia/FoodSaver.

START

The Iditarod begins on Fourth Avenue in downtown Anchorage at 10:00 A.M. on the first Saturday in March. The mushers race 20 miles to Eagle River and then are trucked 29 miles to Wasilla where the race is restarted on Sunday.

Teams leave the restart line in the same order as they left Anchorage. For timing purposes, each musher's total elapsed time is calculated from the restart at Wasilla.

Teams leave the starting line at two-minute intervals in Wasilla, and this time difference is adjusted later at the mandatory 24-hour stop.

Photo: Page 30

STRATEGY

Racing strategies are just as varied and individual as the mushers and their teams. Many mushers purposefully run behind another team, navigating by their scent. However, there are always a few drivers who choose to be the "rabbits" by getting out in front of all the other teams, hoping a storm will come between them and the rest of the teams. The downside of this strategy is that they pave the way and break trail for the rest of the herd. Libby Riddles employed this strategy during her win of the 1985 Iditarod.

Juan Alcina leaves the start line on Anchorage's Fourth Avenue. The race begins the first Saturday in March.
See: START, Page 29

Running grueling races such as the Iditarod and the Yukon Quest involves balancing seemingly opposing strategies. Some believe the key to winning is to disregard the competition, paying attention and making decisions based on your dogs only. Others watch the competition and factor the other teams' situations into their own decisions. And, of course, there is a fine line between pushing dogs too hard, and not pushing them hard enough to let them realize their potential.

Mushers have been known to employ tricks to mislead the competition. Some drivers are notoriously secretive about their strategies and plans. A few go as far as providing false or misleading information to the media and to other drivers. Head games are not always part of the mushing scene, though. Many mushers are friendly and helpful to each other.

Planning and following cycles of run and rest may be the most difficult balancing act. Most mushers try to follow carefully pre-planned cycles of run/rest. If the driver spends too much time resting, he has no chance of winning the race, but if he does not rest enough, the driver or the team may burn out and find themselves scratching from the race.

In the early 1990s, the top racers began using lighter-weight dogs, running faster and faster between checkpoints, and resting more between runs.

Martin Buser swears by his "mental health minute," in which he stops at the team's peak to pet and talk to each individual dog. He insists that this one minute lost is worth many more gained. Most mushers take occasional stops such as these, often to snack the dogs.

Research: Andrea Bachhuber

TIMELINE, 1973-2000

1973: Thirty-six mushers set out from Anchorage in the inaugural race, unsure whether any will reach Nome. Twenty-two people finish. Dick Wilmarth of Red Devil wins the inaugural race in just over 20 days. He never races again. Last place finisher John Schultz records the slowest Iditarod finish ever, more than 32 days. Among the competitors is sprint-dog racing legend George Attla, who finishes fourth. Race founder Joe Redington mortgages his Knik home to get the money for the purse.

1974: Carl Huntington wins in 20 days, 15 hours, becoming the only musher to win both the Iditarod and the Anchorage Fur Rendezvous World Championship sprint race. That record still stands. Joe Redington enters his first race and finishes eleventh, losing a family battle to son Joee Redington, Jr., who is ninth. Mary Shields and Lolly Medley become the first women to finish. Seventeen mushers scratch—41 percent of the starters.

1975: "Yukon Fox" Emmitt Peters of Ruby sets a race record, winning in less than 14 days, 15 hours—about six days faster than the previous year. No musher will finish faster until 1980. Despite Peters' time, his margin of victory is narrow. Jerry Riley of Nenana and Joee Redington are less than an hour behind. Joe Redington records the first of his four fifth-place finishes—his best finish.

1976: Riley wins in almost 18 days, 23 hours to capture the lowest purse in Iditarod history—just $7,200. The man who beat him the previous year, Emmitt Peters, finishes fifth. Brash young rookie Rick Swenson of Manley finishes tenth.

1977: Swenson, who will go on to become the Iditarod's winningest musher, takes the first of five victories in a very tight finish. He beats defending champ Riley by just 5 minutes, and finishes just 17 minutes ahead of Warner Vent. Jon Van Zyle creates the first Iditarod poster to help support the race.

1978: Dick Mackey of Wasilla noses out Swenson in a wild dash down Front Street in Nome. The one-second victory is the closest ever. But at the finish line, there is confusion over who won. Mackey's lead dog crosses the finish line before Swenson's, but Swenson's sled crosses first. Judges rule that in a dog race the first dog wins. Rookie Susan Butcher finishes nineteenth, winning $600. Eventually, her Iditarod winnings will total more than $377,000. William "Sonny" Nelson of Ekwok and all of but two of his dogs are killed in an airplane crash on the way to the race. Nelson's dog handler, James Brandon, races in Nelson's honor.

1979: Swenson becomes the race's first two-time winner, edging Peters by 42 minutes. The race marks a string of near-misses for Peters. Following his championship, he finishes fifth, fourth, third and second in consecutive races. Butcher becomes the first woman to crack the top ten with a ninth-place finish.

1980: Joe May, fifth a year earlier, vaults to the top with a 14-day, 7-hour run—the fastest since Peters' championship in 1975. Among the also-rans are Joe Garnie (twelfth), Larry "Cowboy" Smith (thirteenth), Libby Riddles (eighteenth), Martin Buser (twenty-second) and DeeDee Jonrowe (twenty-fifth). Twenty-five mushers scratch, an Iditarod record.

1981: Ever faster, Swenson and his team win their third victory in 12 days, 9 hours, as the prize money for first place doubles from $12,000 to $24,000. Swenson buddy Sonny Lindner and Roger Nordlum are less than an hour behind. Jeff King manages a twenty-eighth place finish in his rookie run.

1982: Swenson continues his mastery of tight races, beating Susan Butcher to the line by less than 4 minutes. The top three mushers are just 12 minutes apart; the top fifteen are just 11 hours apart. Herbie Nayokpuk, nicknamed "The Shishmaref Cannonball" in honor of his hometown, places twelfth after trying to fight through a blizzard to victory. Other racers sit out the storm in Shaktoolik.

1983: Larry "Cowboy" Smith from Dawson, Yukon Territory, runs alone at the front of the race for hundreds of miles from the Alaska Range to the Bering Sea

coast, where he is caught by Rick Mackey and Eep Anderson. Mackey edges Anderson to become part of the only father-son duo of Iditarod champions (Dick Mackey won the 1978 race). Smith finishes third. Sprint mushing champion Roxy Woods (now Roxy Wright) finishes a disappointing twenty-third in her first Iditarod run.

1984: Dean Osmar of Clam Gulch pioneers a front-running strategy to win the race in just over 12 days, 15 hours after Susan Butcher unexpectedly bolts from the Rohn checkpoint before completing her mandatory 24-hour rest. Osmar says in Rohn that he thinks Butcher has just given him the race. He's right. Butcher finishes second, Joe Garnie (third), Rick Swenson (sixth), Joe Redington (seventh). Defending champion Rick Mackey plummets to twenty-ninth.

1985: Libby Riddles, Garnie's mushing partner from Teller, becomes the first woman to win the Iditarod, charging alone into a fierce storm on Norton Sound.

Her stunning victory brings new attention to the race. In a storm-plagued year, it takes Riddles more than 18 days to reach Nome, the slowest finishing time since 1977. "Was Libby's win important?" asks longtime Iditarod Trail Committeeman Leo Rasmussen of Nome. "To tell you it wasn't would be telling you the greatest lie on earth." Butcher, long expected to be the first woman to win, watches the race from the sidelines after a moose stomps her team on the way to Skwentna.

1986: Butcher wins the first of her four Iditarod victories after a tough battle with Garnie. He finishes second, driving many of the same dogs that produced the championship the year before. With better weather along the trail, forty-five of the fifty-five finishers get to Nome in better time than champion Riddles did the year before.

1987: Butcher knocks about 13 hours off her 1986 time to win again. Swenson pushes her all the way up the Bering Sea Coast, hoping the pressure will make her fold. She doesn't; he does. His dogs refuse to leave the Safety checkpoint. Butcher mushes alone under the burl arch in Nome. Swenson follows her in about 4 hours later. After several futile races with teams of Siberian huskies, future champion Martin Buser of Big Lake breaks into the top ten with a string of Rondy sprint dogs turned marathoners. He finishes in 12 days, 2 hours.

1988: In a dominating display, Butcher completes her trifecta, this time beating Swenson by more than half a day. Buser is third and Garnie fourth. The fourth consecutive victory by a woman leaves fans wondering if a man will ever win again. T-shirts with pithy sayings such as, "Alaska—Where Men Are Men and Women Win

the Iditarod®" are instantly popular. Joe Redington finishes fifth for the fourth time in his career—a remarkable
achievement at age 71.

1989: Butcher leads the race to the halfway point
at Iditarod, but falls victim to what is thought to be a
halfway jinx. Joe Runyan of Nenana, who had dropped
out the previous year, passes her and goes on to win by
68 minutes. Swenson is third, continuing an unmatched
string of top finishes.

1990: Butcher reclaims the championship, her fourth
in five years. Women are back on top. No other Iditarod

musher has ever had a decade of such dominance. "Libby's win started it," said fellow musher DeeDee Jonrowe. "Susan's reign cemented it. They showed it's possible for women to excel on an equal playing field. Libby's win captured the hearts of people who thought only an incredible mountain man could accomplish it."

1991: Swenson battles his way through a White Mountain snowstorm so severe that Butcher, Runyan, and other veterans turn back. It is a record fifth Iditarod win for Swenson. During the worst of it, Swenson leads his team through the storm. Why? "Desperation, I guess," he said. "I wanted to win the Iditarod." Martin Buser manages to fight his way through the same storm, finishing second. Butcher waits for better weather and then leads in a group, including Runyan, who were earlier thought to have a lock on the top positions.

1992: Buser begins his string of three victories, breaking the 11-day barrier and leaving Butcher, Swenson, and Tim Osmar in his wake. Future champion Jeff King breaks into the top ten for the first time with a sixth-place finish.

1993: King vaults to the championship in 10 days, 15 hours, a new record. Jonrowe is 32 minutes behind, and former champion Rick Mackey takes third. Swenson falls to ninth, his worst finish in a decade. Led by Buser and King, the top racers experiment with lighter weight dogs, and a different style of competition, running faster and faster between checkpoints and resting more between runs.

1994: Buser takes his second championship, beating Rick Mackey and defending-champion King. Butcher drops to tenth place and retires after the race. It is her lowest finish since her rookie season of 1978. Swenson climbs back into fourth.

1995: Doug Swingley of Montana makes history, becoming the first non-Alaskan to win the Iditarod in record time—less than 9 days, 3 hours. The top ten mushers make it to Nome in under 10 days.

1996: King captures his second Iditarod, edging Swingley and Buser. A controversy erupts when a Swenson dog dies in harness, the first time Swenson had lost a dog in twenty-one races. Swenson is withdrawn from the race, which leads to a battle with Iditarod officials that has Swenson threatening never to race again. Ultimately, Swenson wins, the rule disqualifying a driver who has lost a dog is rewritten, and Swenson says he will return for the 1998 race.

1997: Buser wins the 25th anniversary Iditarod in less than 9 days, 9 hours to join Swenson and Butcher as the only mushers to win the race at least three times. Swingley is second and King is third. "A bunch of really talented athletes," Buser calls his sixteen-dog team, ten of which finished. Before the race, Buser, 38, had to let go of many of the animals who carried him to his 1992 and 1994 victories. "He was pretty emotionally tied to that team," said his wife, Kathy Chapoton. "A few days before the race he told me this team was better than the 1992 team. That was an incredible thing for him to admit."

1998: Jeff King wins the 26th Iditarod in an official time of 9 days, 5 hours, 52 minutes. DeeDee Jonrowe and Charlie Boulding finish second and third respectively. With previous wins in 1993 and 1996, 1998 is

Doug Swingley

King's third Iditarod victory. King describes the storm during the final strech of the race as the kind of storm "I've only heard described by people. It was the longest couple hours of my life."

1999: Montana musher Doug Swingley wins his second Iditarod title by building a commanding lead at the race's halfway point and never looking back. At 45 years old, Swingley becomes the oldest musher to win the race and only the fifth competitor to win more than one Iditarod. Swingley completed the 27th running of the Iditarod in 9 days, 14 hours, and 31 minutes. Three-time champion Martin Buser arrived in Nome in second place more than 8 hours after Swingley, finishing in 9 days, 23 hours, and 10 minutes.

2000: Doug Swingley's third win is a milestone for him, but he just misses becoming the first musher to run an eight-day Iditarod, at 58 minutes, and 6 second into the ninth day.

Swingley sets a new Iditarod speed record, breaking his own old record (9:2:42:19, set in 1995), and remains the oldest champion (46), and the only musher from Outside (Montana) to win. Swingley's win comes after eluding a chase pack that includes five-time champ Rick Swenson, three-time champs Jeff King and Martin Buser, past Yukon Quest champs Ramy Brooks and Charlie Boulding, and rising star Paul Gebhardt, who finishes second. Swingley receives the first Joe Redington Sr. Trophy, a 95-pound bronze bust named for the Father of the Iditarod, who died in 1999.

Anchorage Daily News, *Mike Campbell*

TRADEMARKS

The following phrases are registered trademarks of the Iditarod Trail Committee:

Iditarod®

The Last Great Race on Earth®

1,049 Miles®

Alaska Where Men Are Men and Women Win the Iditarod®

Iditarod Trail Committee®

Iditarod Days®

Junior Iditarod®

TRAIL MAINTENANCE

In 1972, a race from Anchorage to Nome became more feasible when the U.S. Army reopened much of the trail as a winter training exercise. Volunteer trail breakers did the rest of the work, and the Iditarod Trail became passable.

Today, regular snowmachine and dog team traffic along parts of the trail keeps stretches open throughout the winter, used by villagers for recreation as well as hunting, accessing traplines, and visiting neighboring villages.

The remaining sections of trail are opened and groomed a week or two before the race by volunteer trailbreakers, often villagers living nearby. The trail is marked with four-foot stakes carrying colored reflecting tape so mushers can see them in the dark in the glow of their headlamps.

During the race, a team of trailbreakers using special long-track snowmachines with thousand-pound sleds runs about six hours ahead of the front runners to keep the trail open. That means the lead mushers don't face the disadvantage of wearing out their teams by breaking trail. During bad weather, however, trail conditions can deteriorate so fast that mushers must be able to face any trail condition.

A second team of snowmachiners sweeps the trail after the mushers pass through, picking up trash and dropped equipment, and ensuring the safety of slow-moving mushers.

WEATHER

Weather is hard to predict along the Iditarod Trail in March. Possible temperature extremes range from 45 degrees above zero to 60 degrees below zero (Fahrenheit). Snowfall can vary too, depending on the winter and the region. An average of 80 inches of snow falls annually in the McGrath area, but the Farewell Burn can have patches of open ground. Winds along the Norton Sound can cause a windchill factor of 100 below, and during several races blizzards have halted many mushers and dogs in their tracks.

To keep themselves and their dogs safe, mushers must pay close attention to weather conditions, and most are aware of the following "rules":

30-30-30 rule: at 30 degrees below zero with winds of 30 miles per hour, human flesh freezes solid in 30 seconds.

50-50-50 rule: in water temperature of 50 degrees, a person has 50 percent chance of surviving for 50 minutes.

Section 2

The People

ATKINS, TERRY

The only veterinarian-volunteer on the first Iditarod, Atkins was flown between checkpoints by Joe Redington, Sr. and Art Peterson. Atkins ran his first Iditarod in 1974, after acquiring most of his dogs from the Anchorage dog pound. He started with twelve dogs and all of them were still in the team when he finished, placing nineteenth. He went on to run twenty more Iditarods. He now lives in Sand Coulee, Montana.

AUSTIN, JERRY

Jerry Austin is a three-time winner of the Iditarod's Sportsmanship Award (1987, '89, '93). He has competed eighteen times and finished in the top ten six times, with his best finish in 1982 when he placed third. His fastest time was in 1996 at 10 days, 16 hours, 38 minutes, and 40 seconds.

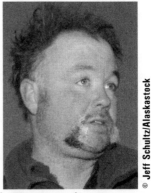

© Jeff Schultz/Alaskastock

Austin is highly regarded by other mushers. In 1989, he and several rookie mushers overtook musher Mike Madden, who was sick and delirious. Austin and another driver mushed to the nearest checkpoint, at night. They contacted ITC headquarters via ham radio. At first light the National Guard sent a helicopter that took Madden to the hospital. Austin then mushed Madden's team the 30 miles into the village. In 1993, he organized and led seventeen other mushers into Nome after they were trapped by weather at White Mountain.

Jerry Austin was named to the Iditarod Hall of Fame in 1997. Born in Seattle, Washington, he lives in St. Michael, Alaska.

BUSER, MARTIN

A three-time winner, Martin Buser was named to the Iditarod Hall of Fame in 1998. He reached Nome first in 1992, 1994, and 1997, with his fastest time coming in 1997 at 9 days, 8 hours, 30 minutes, and 45 seconds. He has run the Iditarod seventeen times through 2000.

Known as a musher who takes outstanding care of his dogs, he has received the Leonhard Seppala Humanitarian Award for dog care four times.

Born in Winterthur, Switzerland, he now lives in Big Lake, Alaska. He got involved in sled dog racing in Europe as a teenager. In 1980, he came to Alaska to run his first Iditarod, finishing twenty-second. It wasn't long before he was back in Alaska for good, liking the wide open spaces and sparse population.

BUTCHER, SUSAN

Named to the Iditarod Hall of Fame in 1997, Susan Butcher was the second woman to win the race. But she didn't stop with her championship in 1986. She followed that win with another in 1987, then again in 1988, then second place in 1989, and first place in 1990. Her fastest time came in 1993, at 10 days, 22 hours, 2 minutes, 40 seconds. Her fastest winning time was in 1990, 11 days, 1 hour, 53 minutes, 23 seconds.

Butcher has run the race seventeen times through 2000, finishing in the top five twelve times and winning more prize money than any other musher. She was the first woman to place in the money, when she crossed the finish line at nineteenth in the 1978 race.

Born in Cambridge, Massachusetts, she now lives near Fairbanks, Alaska.

DELIA, JOE

Joe Delia was named to the Iditarod Hall of Fame in 1997. Though he understands dogs and mushers, Delia has never run the Iditarod.

© Jeff Schultz/Alaskastock

But his home in Skwentna, where he has lived for more than fifty years, has served as the Skwentna checkpoint since the first running of the race in 1973.

Along with his wife, Norma, and a core crew of volunteers numbering twenty-two, they feed and house almost four hundred people each March as the mushers, the media, the race officials, and the spectators pass through.

Delia's own mushing consists of running to the post office and running a trapline. For years, he has put in the trail to and from his checkpoint.

DRUGS AND ALCOHOL, use by mushers

"Use of illegal drugs as defined by state law or excessive use of alcohol by mushers during the race is prohibited. Iditarod has the right to conduct random drug testing. A musher is subject to collection of urine samples at any point from the start until one (1) hour after each team's finish in Nome."

Iditarod Rules, 2001

FATHER OF THE IDITAROD

See: REDINGTON, JOE SR.

FINISHERS

See: APPENDIX III

Jona Van Zyle photo

FIRST WOMAN TO FINISH THE RACE

Mary Shields of Fairbanks, Alaska, in 1974 with lead dog Cabbage (shown here with Ahooah).

FIRST WOMAN TO WIN THE RACE

Libby Riddles, of Teller, Alaska, won the race in 1985 with a time of 18 days, 0 hours, 20 minutes, and 17 seconds. Susan Butcher of Manley, Alaska, then won in 1986, 1987, and 1988, and again in 1990. The success of these women gave rise to the popular T-shirt slogan: "Alaska Where Men Are Men and Women Win the Iditarod," now a registered trademark of the Iditarod Trail Committee.

FIVE-TIME WINNER

Rick Swenson is the only musher to have won the race five times.

FOOD, mushers

Ultimately, a driver's choice of food for himself is his own decision. Items such as frozen pizza and hot dogs seem to be popular. Salami makes a good choice because it is high in fat, contains much protein, and stores well. Honey, chocolate, and high-carbohydrate foods are useful for the energy they produce. Some mushers, mostly Native Alaskans, eat seal oil or bear fat to help them endure cold. Steak and Kentucky Fried Chicken are the choices of others.

The most popular beverages on the trail are water and coffee, although Gatorade and other electrolyte-replenishing sports drinks and the occasional caffeinated soda are popular as well.

According to Mary Hood, author of *Fan's Guide to the Iditarod*, mushers ideally should be chubby, carrying as much as 19 percent body fat, as they have been known to lose as much as 25 to 30 pounds during the race. Most need to consume between 8,000 and 10,000 calories per day to compensate for heat loss and heavy exertion. Pressures of the race and the trail can result in mushers neglecting their own diets, according to Hood—hence the dramatic weight loss.

FOUR-TIME WINNERS

Susan Butcher has won the race four times, topped only by Rick Swenson with five wins.

HALL OF FAME

The *Anchorage Daily News* established the Iditarod Hall of Fame in 1997, to mark the twenty-fifth anniversary of the race. Said Editor Patrick Dougherty, "Our goal was to honor the accomplishments of those whose dedication has made the race legendary."

Nominations come from readers and from a committee established by the *Daily News* and consisting of people with extensive knowledge of the race. Final selections are made by a committee of journalists who have covered the race for many years.

The *Anchorage Daily News* has named the following people to its Hall of Fame:

Jerry Austin	1997	Joe Redington	1997
Susan Butcher	1997	Libby Riddles	1997
Joe Delia	1997	Bob Sept	1997
Dick Mackey	1997	Rick Swenson	1997
Herbie Nayokpuk	1997	Martin Buser	1998
Emmitt Peters	1997	Jeff King	1999

HONORARY MUSHERS

From the Iditarod's first run in 1973 through 1980, Leonhard Seppala, the most famous of the mushers who transported lifesaving diphtheria serum in the historic Nenana-to-Nome run of 1925, was designated as honorary musher, and assigned bib number one.

Each year since then, the Iditarod Trail Committee has selected one or two individuals who have made a significant contribution to the sport, even if he or she is not a musher. The first to receive the honor were the four serum runners still living in the early 1980s: Edgar Nollner, Edgar Kalland, Charlie Evans, and Billy McCarty. In 1992, Herbie Nayokpuk became the only living musher to receive the honor.

Year	Honorary Musher	Year	Honorary Musher
1973 to '79	Leonhard Seppala	1990	Victor "Duke" Kotongan Henry Ivanoff
1980	Leonhard Seppala "Wild Bill" Shannon	1991	"Wild Bill" Shannon Dr. Roland Lombard
1981	Edgar Kalland	1992	Herbie Nayokpuk
1982	Billy McCarty	1993	Leroy Swenson Mike Merkling
1983	Charles Evans Edgar Nollner	1994	Dick Tozier Mike Merkling
1984	Pete MacMannus Howard Albert	1995	John Komok
1985	William A. Egan	1996	Bill Vaudrin
1986	Fred Machetanz	1997	Dorothy G. Page
1987	Eva Brunell "Short" Seeley	1998	Joel Kottke Lolly Medley
1988	Marvin "Muktuk" Marston	1999	Violet "Vi" Redington George Rae
1989	Otis Delvin "Del" Carter, DVM John Auliye	2000	Joe Redington Sr. Edgar Nollner John Schultz

HUNTINGTON, CARL

Winner of the Iditarod in 1974, its second year, Huntington was the only musher ever to win the Iditarod, the Fur Rendezvous World Championship, and the North American Sled Dog Championship sprint races. He died in October 2000.

Volunteer pilots of the "Iditarod Air Force" are key to moving food, supplies, people, and dogs.

IDITAROD AIR FORCE

The volunteer pilots who fly through some of the nation's worst winter weather to transport food, supplies, people, and dogs along the trail have come to be known as the Iditarod Air Force.

These experienced Alaskan pilots use their own planes, and the Iditarod Trail Committee pays for gas, oil, and insurance (often with donations from specific sponsors).

Author Ted Mattson chronicled stories from these pilots in *Adventures of the Iditarod Air Force* (Epicenter Press).

KING, JEFF

Named to the Iditarod Hall of Fame in 1999, King survived a fierce coastal storm to win the 1998 race, his third victory. In only nine years of racing he won the Iditarod three times (1993, 1996, and 1998), the Yukon Quest in 1989, and the Kuskokwim 300 four times. He posted two of the three fastest times ever recorded in the Iditarod.

© Jeff Schultz/Alaskastock

A former Californian, King moved to Denali Park in 1975 and started mushing dogs, running a trapline, and hauling freight. Soon he began entering races and discovered a love of competitive mushing. Today he and his wife, Donna, operate Goose Lake Kennels from their home.

King first entered the Iditarod in 1981, and finished twenty-eighth. It wasn't until 1991 that he ran again. Through 2000, he has not missed a race.

MACKEY, DICK

Named to the Iditarod Hall of Fame in 1997, Dick Mackey helped organize the first Iditarod and, in 1978, won the closest race ever, beating out Rick Swenson by one second. The two teams raced down Nome's Front Street side by side, after a thousand miles of jockeying for the lead. Mackey's lead dog trotted across the line first, and even though Mackey himself collapsed short of the line when the dogs tangled, the judges ruled that the lead dog's nose was all that counted and Mackey had won.

© Jeff Schultz/Alaskastock

A tireless organizer in the early years of the race, he was also one of the most competitive, never finishing out of the top ten in his first six races. He has also served as race committee president, race manager, trail manager, banquet emcee, and start and finish announcer.

Born in Concord, New Hampshire, he now lives in Nenana, Alaska. His fastest time was his winning run in 1978, 14 days, 18 hours, 52 minutes, 24 seconds. Mackey's son Rick won the race in 1983.

MEDIA COVERAGE

The Iditarod was primarily covered by sports reporters from its first run in 1973 until 1985, when Libby Riddles became the first woman to win the race. Riddles' win—mushing to Nome in the teeth of a blizzard that halted the rest of the field—captured the attention of the nation.

Since then, the Iditarod has been covered by nearly every major news organization around the world, as well as by dozens of Alaskan reporters and photographers representing nearly every newspaper, television station, and radio station across the state.

Covering the Iditarod is no small undertaking for any news organization. Because the Iditarod Air Force carries only ITC personnel (except in emergencies) from checkpoint to checkpoint, news organizations use air taxi companies or charter their own aircraft so their crews can move along the trail on their own schedule. For many years, film, videotapes, and stories were flown back to Anchorage and the larger towns along the trail.

The advent of computer-aided communications such as e-mail and websites, along with digital cameras and cam-corders, means most information and images are transported electronically in digital form. Now, information, stills, audio, and video reports are easily found on the internet during the race.

Nevertheless, reporters and photographers still face many of the same logistical and safety challenges as do the mushers along the trail. But instead of keeping dogs safe and warm, they must baby their cameras and computers as they talk with and photograph the mushers and their dogs.

MOTHER OF THE IDITAROD
See: PAGE, DOROTHY G.

MUSHER CONDUCT

Mushers must follow strict rules of conduct as spelled out in the race rules (see Appendix II), including: Good Samaritan Rule; interference; food and gear at checkpoints; passing; sportsmanship; parking; accommodations; litter; use of drugs and alcohol; demand for food and shelter; outside assistance; lost food; No Man's Land; one musher per team; killing of game animals; ELTs or satellite tracking devices, and navigation.

MUSHER QUALIFICATIONS

Mushers must be 18 years of age as of the starting date of the race. A rookie musher (one who has not completed a previous Iditarod) must have completed two approved qualifying races with an accumulated total of at least 500 miles or must have completed one race of at least 800 miles within the last five racing seasons and a 300-mile race in either the current or previous racing season.

A musher must complete any qualifying race and finish in the top 75 percent of the field or in an elapsed time of no more than 200 percent more than the elapsed time of the race winner.

Iditarod Rules, 2001

MUSHER'S PRAYER

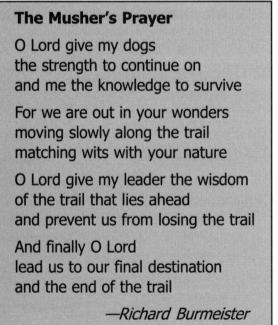

The Musher's Prayer

O Lord give my dogs
the strength to continue on
and me the knowledge to survive

For we are out in your wonders
moving slowly along the trail
matching wits with your nature

O Lord give my leader the wisdom
of the trail that lies ahead
and prevent us from losing the trail

And finally O Lord
lead us to our final destination
and the end of the trail

—Richard Burmeister

Iditarod Silver, *Epicenter Press*

NAYOKPUK, HERBIE

© Jeff Schultz/Alaskastock

Herbie Nayokpuk of Shishmaref, Alaska, on the Bering Sea coast, was named to the Iditarod Hall of Fame in 1997. Known as the Shishmaref Cannonball, Nayokpuk has never won the Iditarod but has finished in the top ten in eight of his eleven races. In 1992, he was the first living musher chosen to wear the Iditarod's honorary bib number one.

He is admired as a musher's musher—respected and liked on the trail and in the dog yard. In 1983, he finished fourth, despite having had open-heart surgery five months earlier. His best finish was second, in 1980. His fastest time was in 1981, 12 days, 22 hours, 17 minutes, 45 seconds. In 1988, he was selected as the Most Inspirational Musher.

OFFICIAL ARTIST
See: VAN ZYLE, JON

OFFICIAL PHOTOGRAPHERS

Jeff Schultz and Jim Brown are official race photographers.

ORGANIZERS

The Iditarod Trail Committee is a nonprofit corporation that relies on volunteers and donations to put together a major event each year. The permanent staff, based in Wasilla, consists of a handful of people, including the full-time race director and part-time race manager. The staff is supplemented by several thousand volunteers. Annual budget for the race is roughly $2 million, which covers the purse, operating expenses, overhead, and shipping food and supplies (as much as 200,000 pounds) to checkpoints.

A race marshal is the top race official and is usually someone with extensive experience in dog mushing and racing. He or she is assisted by a staff of race judges.

At each checkpoint, race personnel include the checker, usually a local resident who often is also a musher. The checker records the official time and number of dogs in the team and in the baskets, and checks required gear. Others may assist the checker, especially if the teams are closely spaced as they arrive. At least three veterinarians are at each checkpoint, and they examine each dog. Other race personnel at each checkpoint handle communications and logistics.

Volunteer trailbreakers ride snowmachines about six hours ahead of the mushers, breaking the trail and where necessary marking it with four-foot pieces of wooden lath with colored reflecting tape. The Iditarod Trail Committee pays their expenses.

In Anchorage and Nome, volunteers put together pre- or post-race banquets and social events, handle the publicity, care for dropped dogs, staff the telephones, operate concession stands, solicit donations, work with sponsors, work with city, state, and federal agencies, and perform dozens of other tasks—small and large—required to put on such a major event.

A musher feeds his dogs; mushers must care for their teams with no outside help during the race.

OUTSIDE ASSISTANCE

"A musher may not receive outside assistance between checkpoints. All care and feeding of dogs will be done only by that team's musher. No planned help, including verbal assistance (i.e. coaching) is allowed throughout the race, at or between checkpoints. All dog maintenance and care of dog teams and gear in checkpoints will be done in the designated localized holding area only. A musher relinquishing the care of his team to leave checkpoint and or village must withdraw from the race. Penalty for infraction of this rule will be either time penalty or disqualification."

Iditarod Rules, 2001

PAGE, DOROTHY G.

Dorothy G. Page became known as the "Mother of the Iditarod" after she successfully promoted the idea of holding a sled dog race as part of the 1967 celebration of the 100th anniversary of Alaska's purchase from Russia.

© Jeff Schultz/Alaskastock

She presented the possibility of a race over the Iditarod Trail to an enthusiastic Joe Redington, Sr. After two short races along the Iditarod Trail in 1967 and 1969, the idea burgeoned and the first Iditarod from Anchorage to Nome took place in 1973.

Page recognized the important role dog mushing played in Alaska's early days and wanted to foster an awareness of sled dogs as working animals and of the Iditarod Trail and the important part it played in Alaska's history.

Editor of the *Iditarod Runner* magazine for many years, Page died at her Wasilla, Alaska, home on November 16, 1989. At the time of her death, she was treasurer of the Iditarod Trail Committee and was active in the Wasilla-Knik-Willow Creek Historical Society. She also served as curator of the Wasilla Museum. From 1975-1989, she wrote and published the *Iditarod Annual* each year.

PEDALING

Pushing the sled with one foot while the other remains on the runner.

PETERS, EMMITT

Named to the Iditarod Hall of Fame in 1997, Emmitt Peters cut six full days off the race when he won in 1975, setting a speed record that stood for five years. Born in Ruby, Alaska, where he still lives, Peters grew up mushing. Instead of just camping and mushing along the Iditarod Trail, he devised strategies for resting and running—strategies that took him to Nome in record time the third year of the race. For the next five years he finished in the top ten, earning the nickname "The Yukon River Fox."

© Jeff Schultz/Alaskastock

Known for the advice and encouragement he gave to rookies, he was popular with his fellow mushers. Peters was unable to maintain his competitive edge after shattering his knee in a training accident in 1986. However, he has continued his involvement with the Iditarod as the checker in Ruby.

His fastest time was in 2000, 12 days, 2 hours, 42 minutes, and 40 seconds. His winning time in 1975 was 14 days, 14 hours, 43 minutes.

PILOTS
See: IDITAROD AIR FORCE

QUOTES

"You could run this race twenty-five years in a row and never figure out how the dogs do it—how they run

a thousand miles in ten or twelve days just because you've asked them to. I want to thank Al, Kennedy, Zack, Ranger, Rusty, Rudy, Cinder, and Zero." **Tim Mowry, Fairbanks. Completed the Yukon Quest eight times and the Iditarod Trail Sled Dog Race twice.**

"Sprint racing is extremely addictive. Worse than cocaine and just as expensive." **Dori Hollingsworth, Seward, sprint musher.**

"A lot of people base too much on their first impression of a dog. The first impression isn't necessarily going to be accurate. A little bit shy doesn't mean the dog doesn't have a strong head. A dog that shows early promise as a leader may not have his head together." **Peter Butteri, Tok, Alaska. Completed the Yukon Quest six times.**

"Mushers like to think of themselves as more important than they are. Humans are but one factor in the training program. The dogs teach each other more than the humans do." **John Wood, Anchorage, sprint musher.**

Rick Mackey's 1998 Yukon Quest leader, Cindy, was taking the team through Fortymile country in her second Quest when she approached a closed-up cabin that had been a checkpoint a year earlier. There were no markers or broken trail. And yet the young dog remembered the place and tried to pull in. That taught Mackey this: "Trust your leaders and you'll stay out of trouble. They know where they're going . . . or at least where they went last year!"

"From running dogs I've learned how the different parts of a team work together. You've got lead dogs, wheel dogs, swing dogs, and team dogs, and they all have to fulfill their particular function for the team to do well. Just like in life, we all have our part." **Daryl Hollingsworth, Seward, sprint musher.**

"It's like a coach on a ball team. You've got to put the players in the right positions, work with them, get the most out of what you've got to work with. It's a challenge to put all these individuals together and make a competitive team." **Joee Redington, Jr., Knik, Alaska, sprint and distance musher.**

"The dogs have as much pride as any human athlete. That's why Granite was a wonderful dog. He knew when he won. He thought he deserved all the accolades, he expected them. He was a ham in front of the media." **Susan Butcher, Fairbanks, four-time Iditarod champion.**

"They know your innermost thoughts. My old lead dog Pal knew more about me than I knew about him." **Roy Monk, Lancashire, England, Iditarod musher.**

"My dogs taught me to shut up and let them do their job. On one run, I talked to my leader Socks the whole time, and finally he laid down and wouldn't get up until I shut up." **Kimarie Hanson, Anchorage, raced in the 1998 Iditarod at age 18.**

"I started with five adults, five pups, one three-legged dog, one borrowed dog, and a coyote. They were moving so slow, by the finish the puppies had grown up." **John Schandelmeier, Paxson, Alaska, Yukon Quest musher.**

"Never eat orange slices with the same gloves you wear to feed the dogs their fish snacks." **Linda Joy, Willow, Iditarod musher.**

Here's how **Jim Lanier, a distance musher from Chugiak**, learned that when all is said and done, dogs will be dogs: "One real 'lowlight' of my mushing experience is when I was taking my team on a training run, and the entire team, one by one, ran through a small door and into a chicken coop. Each dog came out with a squawking chicken in its mouth."

Lessons My Sled Dog Taught Me, *Epicenter Press*

REDINGTON, JOE, SR.

Joe Redington, Sr. was born in Oklahoma on the Chisholm Trail and grew up during the Depression—homeless, motherless, roaming the country looking for work as a field hand. Alaska was his rebirth in 1948. Redington found the home he had never had. On his own piece of dirt, a man could raise a family, hunt, fish, run dogs, and stand up for what he believed.

Redington, his wife, Vi, and their children homesteaded at Flat Horn Lake and in Knik. He has been a big-game guide, a Bush pilot, a miner, and a commercial fisherman, but above all he loved dog mushing. At its peak his kennel housed 500 huskies.

© Jeff Schultz/Alaskastock

Almost single-handedly, Redington rescued Alaska dog mushing from extinction. Seeing dogs disappearing in villages across the state and the snowmachine appearing, he felt something had to be done. With ambition, his abiding love for sled dogs, and refusal to accept "it can't be done," Redington created a legacy in a thousand-mile race across Alaska, and earned the title, "Father of the Iditarod." Redington was named to the Iditarod Hall of Fame in 1997. He ran the race nineteen times—every year from 1974 to 1992. His best finish was fifth, in 1975, 1977, and 1978. His fastest time was in 1989, 12 days, 2 hours, 57 minutes, 16 seconds. He was chosen Most Inspirational in 1988, 1989, and 1997, and received the Sportsmanship Award in 1990.

In 1979 he and fellow Iditarod musher Susan Butcher took a team of seven huskies to the top of 20,320-foot Mount McKinley.

Redington mushed his last Iditarod in 1997, finishing in thirty-sixth place. The year marked the fiftieth year he had mushed on the trail and the twenty-fifth anniversary of the race.

Redington died June 24, 1999, at the age of 82. After his death, a new award was created in his honor, a bronze bust awarded for the first time to Doug Swingley in 2000. The Regal Alaskan Hotel, one of the Iditarod sponsors, renamed its main ballroom after him. He was buried just as he lived—in a dog sled. And at ITC board meetings, his name is still listed for roll call; he is excused as "out on the trail."

RIDDLES, LIBBY

Named to the Iditarod Hall of Fame in 1997, Libby Riddles was the first woman to win the Iditarod. In 1985, she mushed out of Shaktoolik into a blizzard that had stopped every other musher. Three days later, she reached Nome, winning the race in 18 days, 20 minutes and 17 seconds. She has run the race six times, scratching once and recording her best time, 12 days, 8 hours, 34 minutes, 44 seconds, in 1989, when she finished sixteenth

Riddles' win captured the attention of the nation. She received a congratulatory telegram from President Ronald Reagan, *Vogue* ran her photo, The Women's Sports Foundation named her Professional Sportswoman of the Year, and taxi drivers in Nome gave her free rides.

Libby Riddles never won another Iditarod. Born in Madison, Wisconsin, she now lives in Knik, Alaska.

ROOKIE

A musher who has not completed a previous Iditarod. To enter the race, a rookie must have completed two approved qualifying races with an accumulated total of at least 500 miles or must have completed one race of at least 800 miles within the last five racing seasons and a 300-mile race in either the current or previous racing season.

Iditarod Rules, 2001

SCHULTZ, JEFF

Jeff Schultz has been one of the official photographers of the Iditarod Trail Sled Dog Race since 1982, donating his time, energy, and talent to the event each year. An Alaskan since 1978, Schultz grew up in the San Francisco area, where he nurtured a love of the outdoors and photogra-

Clark Mishler Photo

phy. As a boy, he dreamed of building a log cabin and living off the land. At 18, he followed his dream north and launched his career as an outdoor photographer. Since then, Schultz's images have appeared worldwide in advertisements, books, corporate publications, and magazines, among them *National Geographic, Outside,* and *Sports Illustrated.*

Schultz owns and operates Alaska Stock Images, representing more than one hundred photographers. He and his wife, Joan, and their two children, Ben and Hannah, make their home in Anchorage.

SEPPALA, LEONHARD

The most famous of the Serum Run mushers from 1925, Leonhard Seppala was named as the Iditarod's

Leonhard Seppala became the best-known of the 1925 Serum Run mushers.

honorary musher each year from 1973 to 1980, and bib number one was reserved for him

Seppala was one of the top racing mushers in the early part of this century. In 1915, 1916, and 1917, he won the All-Alaska Sweepstakes, a 408-mile race from Nome to Council and back, started in 1908 and run ten times before it was interrupted by World War I. He won a number of other races in Nome and Ruby, and in New England where he began racing in 1927.

In the 1925 serum run, he mushed one of the most difficult legs, with his lead dog Togo in front of the team. Setting out from Nome, they met Myles Gonangnan at Shaktoolik, then turned around and carried the serum to Golovin, 91 miles, travelling a total distance of 260 miles.

Throughout his life, Seppala was an enthusiastic supporter of dog mushing and racing, both in Alaska and in New England, always seeking innovations in styles, techniques, equipment, breeding, and training.

He died in 1967 at the age of 90.

A new high school in Nome is named for Seppala.

SEPT, BOB

© Jeff Schultz/Alaskastock

Veterinarian Dr. Bob Sept was named to the Iditarod Hall of Fame in 1997. He has donated hundreds of hours of veterinary care to the dogs who run the race, never entering it himself. He served as chief veterinarian in 1981 and 1982.

Sept's love of the race runs deep, leading him to take over as race president in 1983 when the Iditarod was ailing—in debt, understaffed, and overwhelmed. Sept led the race out of debt and onto a solid footing. When Libby Riddles' win in 1985 captured the attention of the nation and a broader audience, he was able to return to his veterinary duties, continuing to help improve the care of dogs and the rules governing their treatment.

Born in Pocatello, Idaho, he lives in Chugiak, Alaska.

SERUM RUN MUSHERS, 1925

Musher	Leg of Serum Rum	Miles
"Wild Bill" Shannon	Nenana to Tolovana	52
Edgar Kalland	to Manley Hot Springs	31
Dan Green	to Fish Lake	28
Johnny Folger	to Tanana	26
Sam Joseph	to Kallands	34
Titus Nickoli	to Nine Mile Cabin	24
Dave Corning	to Kokrines	30
Harry Pitka	to Ruby	30
Billy McCarty	to Whiskey Creek	28
Edgar Nollner	to Galena	24
George Nollner	to Bishop Mountain	18
Charlie Evans	to Nulato	30
Tommy Patson	to Kaltag	36
Jack Screw	to Old Woman	40
Victor Anagick	to Unalakleet	34
Myles Gonangnan	to Shaktoolik	40
Henry Ivanoff	to meeting with Seppala	
Leonhard Seppala*	to Golovin	91
Charlie Olson	to Bluff	25
Gunnar Kaasen	to Nome	53

*Seppala set out from Nome, met Ivanoff outside Shaktoolik, turned around and carried the serum to Golovin, 91 miles, but travelling a total distance of 260.

SPORTSMANSHIP

"Any musher must use civil conduct and act in a sportsmanlike manner throughout the race. Abusive treatment of anyone is prohibited."

Iditarod Rules, 2001

STOVE UP

Injured, generally temporarily; either musher or dog.

SWENSON, RICK

Rick Swenson is the only musher to have won the race five times, reaching Nome first in in 1977, '79, '81, '82, and '91. In 1978, he lost the race by one second when Dick Mackey's lead dog poked his nose over the finish line first.

Known for his steely determination, in 1991 he set out from White Mountain into the teeth of a blizzard that had turned back other mushers. His perseverance paid off and he claimed his fifth victory.

Swenson has finished among the top five mushers sixteen times. His fastest time was in 1995, 9 days, 22 hours, 32 minutes. His fastest winning time was in 1981, 12 days, 8 hours, 45 minutes, 2 seconds

Swenson was born in Willmar, Minnesota, and now lives in Two Rivers, Alaska. He was named to the Iditarod Hall of Fame in 1997.

SWINGLEY, DOUG

Three-time winner Doug Swingley is the only musher living outside Alaska to win the Iditarod, placing first in 1995, 1999, and 2000. A resident of Lincoln, Montana, he was named Rookie of the Year in his first race in 1992.

Swingley began mushing in 1989. He has run the Iditarod each year since '92, always finishing in the top ten.

THREE-TIME WINNERS

Jeff King, Rick Swenson, Susan Butcher, Martin Buser, and Doug Swingley each have won the race at least three times. Swenson has five victories, Butcher four, and Buser, King, and Swingley three.

See also: CHAMPIONS

TOP TEN FINISHERS, 1973-2000

Musher	Top 10 Finishes	Musher	Top 10 Finishes
Rick Swenson	22	Ken Chase	3
Susan Butcher	15	Don Honea	3
Martin Buser	14	"Cowboy" Smith	3
DeeDee Jonrowe	11	Warner Vent	3
Rick Mackey	11	Howard Albert	2
Tim Osmar	10	Ron Aldrich	2
Jeff King	9	John Baker	2
Doug Swingley	9	Ernie Baumgartner	2
Herbert Nayokpuk	8	Guy Blankenship	2
Lavon Barve	8	Ramy Brooks	2
Charlie Boulding	7	Rudy Demoski	2
Vern Halter	7	Matt Desalernos	2
Emmitt Peters	7	Linwood Fiedler	2
Joe Redington, Sr.	7	Paul Gebhardt	2
Jerry Austin	6	Robin Jacobson	2
Bill Cotter	6	Peryll Kyzer	2
Dick Mackey	6	Joe May	2
Joe Runyan	5	Roger Nordlum	2
Eep Anderson	4	Robert Schlentner	2
John Cooper	4	Dan Seavey	2
Joe Garnie	4	Mitch Seavey	2
Duane Halverson	4	Sven Engholm	1
Sonny Lindner	4	Ed Iten	1
Jerry Riley	4	David Sawatzky	1
Terry Adkins	3	Raymie Smyth	1

VAN ZYLE, JON

Jon Van Zyle is an internationally recognized wildlife artist closely identified with sled dog racing in his home state of Alaska.

Twice Van Zyle has run the Iditarod Trail Sled Dog Race from which he derived artistic inspiration for a magnificent series of original paintings,

Charlotte Van Zyle photo

prints, and posters that capture the excitement and spirit of the annual race. He has been designated as race's official artist.

More than two hundred of his works have been published as limited edition prints and posters in the last twenty-some years. Van Zyle, who lives in a cedar home near Eagle River, Alaska, owns a team of Siberian huskies that he runs with his wife, Jona, also a musher and an artist and author.

In 1979, he was named Official Iditarod Artist, a title he cherishes and still holds. Each year he donates a portion from the proceeds of the Iditarod poster and Iditarod print sales to help support the race. The 2001 poster marks the twenty-fifth anniversary of the official Iditarod posters. A book titled *Jon Van Zyle's Iditarod Memories*, written by his wife Jona, commemorates this event.

In the past twenty-five years, Jon has created hundreds of acrylic paintings and stone lithographs that express the beauty of Alaska's wilderness and wildlife, and his love of nature.

VAUGHAN, NORMAN

At the age of 88, Vaughan finished the race for the fourth time in 1990; he led an expedition to Antarctica in the winter of 1993-'94.

© Jeff Schultz/Alaskastock

Vet Caroline Griffitts examines a dog at Nikolai. All dogs get a vet check at each checkpoint.

VETERINARIANS

About thirty-five volunteer veterinarians monitor the health and welfare of dogs racing in the Iditarod. Just as the dogs and mushers must meet certain qualifications, so must the vets, including five years in practice and previous experience working with racing sled dogs.

Veterinarians are selected in August. The chief vet makes optional kennel visits before the race. Pre-race veterinary work includes microchipping, vaccinations, deworming, pre-race veterinary physical exams within 10 days of the race start, EKGs, blood work, and making sure each musher has completed Dog Care Agreement Forms.

During the race, the veterinarians examine the dogs at checkpoints. Mushers are required to carry dog-care diaries which serve as written medical records for the dogs and can be examined by vets. Vets also conduct random drug testing as a precaution, monitor dropped dog care, and determine cause of death for any dogs that die during the race.

In addition to looking out for the dogs before and during the race, many vets conduct medical studies, including research on gastro-intestinal disorders and vitamin deficiency.

VOLUNTEERS

Working with the staff of the Iditarod Trail Committee are hundreds of volunteers and silent supporters who labor behind the scenes—as many as 1,500 in any given year. For every mile of trail, someone is helping with a task. The obvious supporters are the sponsors of the race and of the competitors; however, there are many more tasks performed that largely go unnoticed. The trail is laid down and marked every year by Iditarod trail breakers on snowmachines, as well as local volunteers working on sections near their villages.

Among the hundreds of volunteers who help each year are those preparing food for shipment.

Others help with the 60 to 100 tons of trail supplies, straw for the dogs, tents, fuel, and food for the checkpoints. Every item is handled many times, from initial pick-up to final delivery to some of the most remote places in Alaska. Several thousand dog exams are performed, from the pre-race at headquarters, to team checks along the trail, to the final health exam after the finish line.

It takes more than two hundred volunteers in Anchorage to get the start off, and about the same for the restart in Wasilla.

During the race, two hundred to three volunteers at race headquarters at the Regal Alaskan Hotel answer phones and e-mail, input race statistics into computers, manage race communications, sell merchandise, handle arrangements for dropped dogs, and perform myriad other tasks.

In Nome for the finish, in addition to local residents, at least fifty people pay their own way there to volunteer at headquarters, sell merchandise, make banquet arrangements, help in the dog lot and more.

In 2000, more than three hundred volunteers came from other states and countries to help.

Some of the volunteers come back year after year; for others it is a once-in-a-lifetime experience. All are working for a common cause: the dogs.

WOMEN

Sled dog racing is unique in that it is one of the few sports in which men and women compete on an equal footing. While training and fitness are important, sound judgment, experience, and drive tend to be the more important qualities in a musher. No women raced in the first Iditarod of 1973, but the following year, Mary Shields and Lolly Medley entered, and both completed the race.

Slowly, the Iditarod began increasing its popularity with women. In 1980, seven women entered the race, and all but one completed it. Two years later, in 1982, Susan Butcher placed second, and the following year ten women entered the race, with only one scratching. In 2001 fourteen women entered.

The first woman to win the Iditarod was Libby Riddles, who won in 1985 by continuing on through a storm while all the others waited it out. Susan Butcher, after placing second in 1982 and in 1984, won the Iditarod in 1986, 1987, 1988, and 1990.

The Dogs

© Jeff Schultz/Alaskastock

Balto, a lead dog in the 1925 Serum Run, was memorialized with a statue in New York's Central Park.

BALTO

Balto was a lead dog owned by Leonhard Seppala, the most famous of the mushers who transported lifesaving diphtheria serum to Nome in 1925. Though owned by Seppala, Balto led Gunnar Kaasen's team and the serum into Nome. He became a high-profile dog hero memorialized with a statue in New York's Central Park. Seppala's own lead dog was Togo. After his death, Balto, along with Togo, was custom mounted. Balto is on display at the Cleveland, Ohio, Museum of Natural History. Togo's permanent home is at Iditarod headquarters in Wasilla, Alaska.

Iditarod Silver, *Epicenter Press*

See also: TOGO

BREEDS

Most dogs who race are considered to be "Alaskan Huskies," a breed not yet recognized by the American Kennel Club. More of a lineage than a breed, the Alaskan Husky is a mixed breed that has been bred for stamina, intelligence, power, and speed. It is often a mix between the Siberian Husky and other breeds.

Racing dogs usually weigh 40 to 60 pounds. In the early days of the Iditarod, dogs used in long-distance races tended to be larger, in some cases weighing as much as 70 pounds while sprint dogs were in the 40-pound range. New racing strategies have resulted in some mushers using lighter dogs for distance racing.

One strain of Alaskan Husky is the Aurora Husky, developed by Gareth Wright. His dogs are said to be one-half Siberian Husky, one-quarter wolf, and one-quarter Irish Setter. Other strains of Husky developed in Alaska include the Mackenzie River Husky and the Huslia Husky. Whatever one chooses to call them, the dogs are bred for endurance and speed. Many serious mushers keep their own kennels, manipulating and propagating their own unique strains of racing dogs as they see fit.

More exotic breeds have been mushed in the Iditarod, however. John Suter, known as the Poodle Man, has raced a string of standard poodles. Current rules stipulate that only northern dog breeds suitable for arctic travel will be permitted to enter the race. "Northern breeds" will be determined by race officials.

COME GEE! COME HAW!

Commands for 180-degree turns in either direction.

© Jeff Schultz/Alaskastock

The lean huskies used for sprint racing are bred for speed and usually weigh about 40 pounds.

© Jeff Schultz/Alaskastock

In early years distance racers used heavier dogs weighing up to 60 pounds; now lighter dogs are also used.

DOG BREEDS
See: BREEDS

DOG DEATHS

With more than 1,000 dogs on the trail at the start of each race, it is inevitable that dogs will die, despite the extreme care taken to ensure their health and safety.

Iditarod rules require that "any dog that expires on the trail must be taken by the musher to a checkpoint. The musher may transport the dog to either the checkpoint just passed, or the upcoming checkpoint.

"An expired dog report must be completed by the musher and presented to a race official along with the dog.

"The chief veterinarian will cause a necropsy to be carried out by a board certified pathologist at the earliest opportunity and shall make every attempt to determine the cause of death. If a board-certified pathologist is not available to perform the necropsy within the time frame to preserve the tissues appropriately, (as determined by the race marshal), the gross necropsy and tissue collection will be performed by a trail veterinarian following the guidelines in the Musher and Veterinary Handbook. These tissues will then be examined by a board-certified pathologist. The race marshal or his/her appointed judges, will determine whether the musher should continue or be disqualified."

A musher will be disqualified if a dog dies with signs of cruel, inhumane, or abusive treatment or the cause of death is heat stress, or hyperthermia.

Iditarod Policies and Iditarod Rules, 2001

© Jeff Schultz/Alaskastock

Martin Buser with a dog in the basket. Dogs are carried there if they are injured or tired.

DOG IN BASKET

Tired or injured dog carried in the sled.

DOUBLE LEAD

Two dogs who lead the team side by side.

DROPPED DOGS

When a dog is injured, fatigued, or becomes ill, a musher may "drop" or remove it from the team. Race rules require that "all dogs that are dropped from the race must be left at a designated dog drop area with a completed and signed dropped dog form. Any dropped dog must be left with four (4) pounds of dog food and a reliable chain or cable (16" to 18" in length) with swivel snap and collar."

Dogs dropped at checkpoints may be moved to the closest dog collection area. These are Anchorage, McGrath, Galena, Unalakleet, and Nome.

Eventually, dropped dogs are returned to Anchorage, either by the musher or the ITC, where they are collected by the musher or his handlers.

Iditarod Policies and Iditarod Rules, 2001

DRUG USE, on dogs

"No injectable, oral or topical drug which may suppress the signs of illness or injury may be used on a dog. A musher may not inject any substance into their dogs. No other drugs or other artificial means may be used to drive a dog or cause a dog to perform or attempt to perform beyond its natural ability."

The following drugs are prohibited:

A. Anabolic Steroids

B. Analgesics (prescriptive and non-prescriptive)

C. Anesthetics

D. Antihistamines

E. Anti-inflammatory drugs including but not limited to:
    1. Cortico-steroids (the exception is for use on feet)
    2. Antiprostaglandins
    3. Non-steroidals
    4. Salicylates
    5. DMSO

F. Bronchodilators

G. Central Nervous System Stimulants

H. Cough Suppressants

I. Diuretics

J. Injectable Anticolinergics

K. Muscle Relaxants

L. Tranquilizers & Opiates

Iditarod Rules, 2001

FOOD, dogs

A sled dog is fed a diet very different than the average house dog because its nutritional requirement is so different. The average long-distance sled dog consumes more than 11,000 calories per day when racing, compared to a diet of 2,500 calories per day in a kennel.

On the trail, dogs eat at meal time and at snack time. Full meals are usually the mushers' own personal mix, emphasizing proteins such as liver, fats and oils, and other nutrients. This food is warmed before it is fed to the dogs.

Emmitt Peters of Ruby, who set a new record with his 1975 Iditarod win, "cooked up green fish [frozen fish], beef tallow, and rice, put it in plastic bags and froze it." This, "along with five pounds of commercial dog food and two pounds of honey" and "beaver meat and beef" fed his dogs during the length of the Iditarod. (*Iditarod Silver*, Epicenter Press)

Iditarod musher Joe May became an advocate of fishmeal and oil in dogs' diets. Some drivers choose to add eggs for protein and fat. Other items are cream cheese, honey, brewer's yeast, bonemeal for its calcium and minerals, and cottage cheese which is said to improve muscle tone. Fats and oils may come from corn oil, canola oil, fish oil, seal oil, vegetable oil, safflower oil, wheat germ oil, chicken, turkey, beef, beaver, seal blubber, and the tallow from meat scraps.

Snacks are fed cold to the dogs quickly on a break.

© Jeff Schultz/Alaskastock

Bags of race supplies and dog food, packed and frozen before the race, await each musher at some checkpoints.

Common snacks include whitefish and water, sometimes with gelatin or canned dog food added, and salmon, whitefish, herring or other fish mixed with vegetable, corn, flax, or coconut oil. Frozen snacks contain much-needed water to help avoid dehydradation.

Mushers prepare the dogs' food prior to the race, freeze it, and the ITC ships it to the checkpoints in containers weighing no more than 70 pounds.

Research: Andrea Bachhuber

GEE

Command for right turn.

HAW

Command for left turn.

HUSKY

Any northern-type dog.

INDIAN DOG

An Alaskan husky from an Indian village.

INJURIES, dog

As with any athlete in a grueling event, sled dogs can be injured. In recent years, sled dog racing has been criticized by animal rights' organizations that claim it causes the dogs unnecessary suffering. Mushing supporters point out that with proper care and necessary precautions, sled dogs are no more prone to disease or injury than any house pet.

Among injuries that may befall a sled dog are generalized crippling, localized crippling, muscle or tendon tears, disc syndrome, cramping, dislocations, fractures, ice balling, broken toenails, worn nails, worn or torn footpads, and dehydration. Viruses may also strike a team.

Dehydration is of special concern in distance races (for both dogs and mushers). Up to 60 percent of a dog's weight is water, and it is depleted by exercise. The colder and windier it is, the more likely the dog will experience dehydration. To combat this, mushers heat the dogs' water, sometimes adding meat or chicken broth. On the trail each dog will need as much as a gallon of water per day.

Dogs can lose all of their body fat and half of their protein and still function, but if they lose even 20 percent of their water, inevitably death will result.

Although the death of racing dogs is an uncommon tragedy—less than one-third of 1 percent of sled dogs will die in training or competition (fewer than one out of three hundred dogs)—several different circumstances can result in a dog's death. These include gastric torsion (twisted stomach), burst blood vessels in the brain, and dehydration.

To ensure the dogs' health and well-being, the Iditarod requires pre-race veterinary screenings, which include urine tests for prohibited drugs. All dogs entered in the race must have current distemper, parvo, corona and rabies vaccines, and all teams must be dewormed for Echinoccocus Multilocularis.

Veterinary checks also are made along the trail, and mushers are required to carry a veterinarian notebook, to be presented to the veterinarian at each checkpoint.

LEAD DOG OR LEADER

The dog that runs in front of the team pulling the sled. Often the lead dog is the musher's best friend and most reliable dog. Lead dogs must be intelligent and fast. Sometimes a pair of dogs will run in double lead.

LINE OUT

Command for lead dog to pull the team out straight from the sled. Used mostly while hooking dogs into team or unhooking them.

MALAMUTE

This larger, stronger dog is often used for freighting. The name is derived from the Malamutes, Alaska Natives living at the mouth of the Yukon River. The American Kennel Club's list of recognized breeds includes the Alaskan Malamute, which may weigh up to 75 pounds.

MUSH! HIKE! ALL RIGHT! LET'S GO!

All are commands to start the team. "Mush," though frequently found in story and song, is rarely used by mushers (the term "mushers" came from the French *marché*, to march or go forward).

SIBERIAN HUSKY

This medium-sized (average 50 pounds) northern breed of dog is recognized by the American Kennel Club, unlike the Alaskan Husky, which is a lineage rather than a breed.

As its name implies, the Siberian Husky originated in Siberia. It was brought to Alaska in the early 1900s. Originated by the Chukchi people of northeastern Asia, the Siberian Husky was bred as a sled dog, with the endurance and stamina that their semi-nomadic way of life required. Agile, fast, and possessing an incredible endurance, it is a born runner.

The Siberian's height is usually between 20 and 24 inches, and weight between 35 and 60 pounds. As with many breeds, the female tends to be smaller and lighter. A medium-sized, compact, and furry dog, it can be recognized by its beautiful coat that comes in a wide range of colors including black, white, gray, and red. The Siberian's eyes can be blue, brown, or a combination.

Though often stubborn and difficult to train, Siberian Huskies are highly intelligent, a characteristic that leads them to become bored easily and therefore prone to mischief. The American Kennel Club recognized the breed in 1930, leading to a split between dogs bred as show dogs, and dogs bred as sled dogs. Siberian Huskies bred for racing in Alaska in particular have been mixed with other breeds over the years producing a dog known as the Alaskan Husky, not recognized by the AKC.

SWING DOG OR DOGS

Dog that runs directly behind the leader. Further identified as right or left swing depending on which side of the tow line it's placed. Its job is to help "swing" the team in the turns or curves.

TEAM DOG

Any dog other than the leader, wheel dogs, or swing dogs.

TEAM SIZE

"The maximum number of dogs a musher may start the race with is sixteen (16) dogs. A musher must have at least twelve (12) dogs on the line to start the race. At least five (5) dogs must be on the tow line at the finish line. No dogs may be added to a team after the restart of the race. All dogs must be either on the tow line or hauled in the sled and cannot be led behind the sled or allowed to run loose."

Iditarod Rules, 2001

© Jeff Schultz/Alaskastock

TOGO

Togo was one of the lead dogs of Leonhard Seppala, the most famous of the mushers who transported lifesaving diphtheria serum in the historic Nenana-to-Nome run of 1925. Togo took Seppala from Nome to Shaktoolik to Golovin in 1925, crossing Norton Sound through gale winds and 30-below-zero temperatures.

Although another of Seppala's dogs, Balto, who led Gunnar Kaasen's team, became famous, Seppala believed that Togo didn't get his due. Balto ran 53 miles, while Togo ran 260 miles. After their deaths, both Togo and Balto were mounted. Togo's permanent home is at Iditarod headquarters in Wasilla, Alaska.

Before Togo's mount was moved to Alaska in 1983, it was displayed at the Shelbourn Museum in Burlington, Vermont, where it was petted so much, the ears and tail had to be replaced. Now the mount no longer has Togo's distinctive bent right ear tip.

Balto's mount is on display at the Cleveland, Ohio, Museum of Natural History.

Iditarod Silver, *Epicenter Press*

See also: BALTO

TRAIL!

Request for right-of-way on the trail.

TRAINING

Although mushers use different techniques for training their teams, based on experience, finances, location, and size of kennel, most training regimens follow a similar seasonal cycle.

Late spring and summer are the musher's and team's resting periods, or off-season. Training gets more intense throughout the autumn and winter, peaking during the racing season in the winter and early spring.

During the warm temperatures of summer, dogs at large kennels often are exercised on a dog walker or exercise wheel. Attached to an overhead fan-like paddle, the dogs run in circles for 45 minutes at a time. This allows the trainer to determine which of the dogs have the fastest and smoothest gait, as well as keeping the

animals in shape for the upcoming racing season. Another low-impact summertime exercise is swimming, which minimizes the risk of the dogs overheating while keeping them clean and cool.

Puppies are often born during the summer, so the summer months are usually filled with the socialization of puppies. Trainers try to handle the pups' feet frequently so that they will get used to having booties put on and taken off. The trainer also tries to encourage good eating habits from a young age. The puppies are given a relatively short time to eat before their food is removed. This process is repeated over and over until the pups learn to eat what they are fed, when it is offered.

At eight weeks old, the pups are weaned. After that, they are taken on daily walks of one to seven miles, accompanied by one or more adult dogs as role models. The walks help build the puppies' muscle tone, while allowing the trainer to see which pups show promise. Trainers look for puppies willing to go anywhere: through water, over ice, across obstacles. As the puppies grow, the walks get longer. At about six to eight months old, harness training begins with one-half- to one-mile runs.

The trainer is careful never to push the puppies beyond their limits. Good sled dogs must have an innate love of the sport, and trainers never push puppies beyond what they already love and desire to do.

In August more intense training begins. Each dog goes on 3- to 4-mile runs several times a week. While the ground is still dry, the dogs pull wheeled carts, or all-terrain vehicles. Yearling puppies often are paired with more experienced racing veterans, so that they

Jeff King prepares a meal for his dogs; during the race mushers must care for the team without outside help.

might pick up positive traits and habits. Cart training builds the dogs' muscles, gradually getting them into the routine of hard work. It also allows the trainer to teach younger dogs new commands, while reminding the older dogs of commands they already know. The length and frequency of these workouts increase throughout the fall and winter until the dogs reach their optimal physical condition. As with young puppies, the trainer is careful never to drive the dogs to the point where they lose enthusiasm for racing.

As the dogs are trained and taught commands, usually the trainer's tone of voice is enough to encourage them to obey. As they are trained, the dogs must learn not to pull off the trail to lift a leg, or to sniff something interesting. They also must learn to run fast enough and to keep up with the rest of the team. They must learn to keep the tug line tight and to do their fair share of the work. It is here that the musher's mantra of "the team is only as fast as its slowest dog" comes in. The trainer will not tolerate a dog disobeying a command, showing aggression to humans, or fighting with other dogs.

By December, the dogs may be running 25 to 75 miles four or five days per week. The trainer continues to evaluate the dog's performance, deciding which dogs are best for which positions, and which dogs work well together in pairs. Factors affecting pairing matches are height, weight, and gait similarities, as well as personality matches.

By observing their tails, ears, and heads, the driver can recognize which dogs are slacking off, which dogs are tired, and which dogs are under too much stress.

Above all, the trainer is careful to continuously praise his team for jobs well done.

As individual race dates approach, the musher begins to take care of some administrative tasks. Early in the winter, he or she begins assembling food and equipment into bundles that will be sent ahead to each individual checkpoint of mid- and long-distance races. Several weeks before the race, the driver must make the final selection of dogs that will compose the team. For teams entering the Iditarod, by this time the dogs will have completed over 2,000 miles of training, including qualifying mid- or long-distances races in January and February. As the weeks before the race melt away, the dogs are taken on short runs to preserve their muscle tone and to maintain their interest in racing.

As the racing season ends, trainers and drivers begin turning their attention to breeding plans. Spring is the season for rest; soon the whole process will start all over again.

Reseach: Andrea Bachhuber

WHEEL DOG OR WHEELERS

Dogs placed directly in front of the sled. Their job is to pull the sled out and around corners or trees.

WHOA!

Command to halt the team, accompanied by heavy pressure on the brake.

Gear

BASKET

The section of the sled in front of where the musher stands; where gear is stowed on the sled. If dogs weaken, they are carried in the basket to the next checkpoint.

BOOTIES

A type of sock worn by the dogs to protect their feet from small cuts and sores when the trail is icy and rough. These are made of various materials such as denim, polar fleece, or trigger cloth, and usually are held in place with Velcro fasteners. Mushers are required to carry at least eight booties for each dog.

© Jeff Schultz/Alaskastock

A musher puts booties on a dog. Booties protect the dog's feet when the trail is icy or rough.

BRUSH BOW

The semicircular part of the sled frame that serves as a front bumper.

CLOTHING

Most mushers dress in layers, beginning with light underwear—often polypropylene or silk—that wicks moisture away from the skin while providing insulation.

Choices for middle layers include turtlenecks, crewnecks, pullovers, button-ups, vests, sleeved shirts, bibs, and jumpsuits. Materials for this layer include wool, polypropylene, Thermax®, and fleece. Bibs are an insulated pant with shoulder straps and a chest covering, commonly used by snowmachiners. One-piece jumpsuits can be opened to the waist and dropped down (often with the help of suspenders) to avoid overheating during hard work.

The outer shell protects the musher from wind and moisture. It should be waterproof, windproof, warm, lightweight, tear-resistant, breathable, and comfortable. Outer parkas may have an insulated lining and a waterproof outer layer such as nylon laminate. These thigh-length jackets usually include pockets, freeze-resistant zippers, storm flaps, wrist cuffs, and an oversize hood with a fur ruff.

When deciding what materials to use, several considerations are important. Wool is warm, but heavy when wet. Down is light and warm, but useless when wet, and also highly flammable. Venteel® is a popular tight-woven cotton. Gortex®, Thinsulate, and Thermalite are all newer synthetic materials, popular because they are lightweight and windproof. Still, traditional materials

© Jeff Schultz/Alaskastock

Linda Joy is dressed for extreme cold with a heavy parka, knit cap, and wolverine fur-ringed hood.

often are preferred. The Alaska Native combination of animal skins and furs remains popular, as the skin protects against wind while the fur holds in heat.

Two common forms of footwear for dog sled racers are mukluks and bunny boots. Traditionally, knee-high

mukluks were made with hard sealskin soles and caribou fur or moose hide uppers. Without zippers or any
other openings, they were lined with grass and fitted by
wrapping rawhide strips around the leg from the ankle
to the knee. Now they are used with a foam insert. The
major drawback of mukluks is that water seeps through
easily.

Bunny boots are insulated with waterproof rubber
and canvas. Developed by the U.S. Army, their major
advantage is a vapor barrier created by double layered
rubber with an insulating air pocket in-between. Newer
bunny boots made of synthetic materials allow air cir-
culation—old rubber boots tend to result in damp, smelly,
uncomfortable feet if worn too long. This can be pre-
vented by changing socks three or more times a day,
and rubbing a dry-skin cream on the feet to prevent
cracks and splits.

The musher's choice of socks depends on the choice
of boots, ranging from heavy polypropylene, to thick
wool to light liners.

Mushers nearly always wear either mittens or gloves,
or sometimes a combination of both. For instance, mitts
with fur backs and leather palms are often worn with a
light glove inside. Sometimes a musher will employ a
three- or four-layer system of gloves and mittens, with
thin liner gloves of silk or poly closest to the skin, followed by a wool or chore glove over, in turn covered
with overmitts of fur and synthetic open-cell foam. When
it is very cold, a gauntlet extending past the elbow may
be the outer layer.

As up to 50 percent of a person's body heat is lost
through the head and neck, head and face protection is

crucial. Hats made of wolf, fox, or beaver pelt on the outside and wool felt on the inside are common. Parkas with a fur trim around the face opening are popular, too, as they create an insulated layer of air around the face. Wolf or wolverine fur is desirable, as it doesn't frost up and break off. A fleece or poly cap may be worn under the parka hood. Other headgear may include a fleece face mask, a neck gaiter which can be pulled up over the chin and nose, sunglasses, headlamp, leather eye proctors, or even glacier goggles.

EMERGENCY LOCATOR TRANSMITTERS

"While a musher may carry an emergency tracking device, such as an emergency locator transmitter (ELT) or other similar satellite tracking device, activation will make a musher ineligible to continue and will result in withdrawal from the race."

Iditarod Rules, 2001

EQUIPMENT, 1978 list of required equipment to be carried during race

In 1978, mushers were required to carry with them:
1. Proper cold weather sleeping bag.
2. Hand ax.
3. One pair of standard snowshoes with bindings.
4. Any promotional material that the musher has been asked by the committee to carry to Nome.
5. One day's food for each dog, with a minimum of two pounds per dog.
6. One day's food ration for each musher.
7. Two sets of booties for each dog either in the sled, or in use.

© Jeff Schultz/Alaskastock

Equipment is spread out on the snow as Juan Alcina prepares to pack his sled.

EQUIPMENT, current list of required equipment to be carried during race

A musher must have with him/her at all times the following items:

1. Proper cold weather sleeping bag weighing a minimum of 5 pounds

2. Ax, head to weigh a minimum of $1^3/_4$ pounds, handle to be at least 22 inches long.

3. One pair of snowshoes with bindings, each snowshoe to be at least 252 square inches in size.

4. Any promotional material provided by the ITC.

5. Eight booties for each dog, in the sled or in use.

6. One operational cooker and pot capable of boiling at least 3 gallons of water.

7. Veterinarian notebook, to be presented to the veterinarian at each checkpoint.

EQUIPMENT, optional

Every sled bag contains at least one cooler (to keep food hot), bowls for the dogs, ladle, cooking pots, dishes, cups, and utensils for the driver. Many also choose to keep a thermos handy. Although camping gear used to be considered a necessity, few tents are included now. Rather, most mushers choose to sleep in a sleeping bag, often using a waterproof poncho as a ground cloth or cover for moisture protection.

Spare parts may include collars and harnesses, neck line, tug line, and gang line, runner plastic, and other replacement parts. Tools and equipment for repairs may include needles; dental floss; screwdriver; wrenches; extra bolts, nuts, hooks, and snaps; hacksaw blade; and extra wire.

Most mushers carry additional personal and safety supplies, including a headlamp, chemical handwarmers, knife, a complete set of clothes in a waterproof bag, and a simple first aid kit. Other small items may include a space blanket, flashlights, matches, a compass, heat packs, sunglasses, lip salve, energy food, and a survival manual.

Most mushers bring along a few light personal items to make their adventure more comfortable and enjoyable. Common choices are a tape or CD player and headphones, a notebook and pencil, a camera and film, and personal hygiene supplies such as soap, toothbrush and toothpaste, comb and brush, razors and shaving supplies, and pre-moistened wipes. An extra pair of glasses or contact lenses are almost a necessity. Savvy mushers bring small portable alarm clocks to wake them at checkpoints. Many drivers bring postcards, musher cards, trading or collector cards, and other small items for fans and checkpoint residents.

GANG LINE

The main line running down the center of the dog team to front of the sled, the gang line (also called tow line) is the heaviest, longest rope at 3/8 to 1/2 inch diameter. The number of sections of gang line is determined by the number of dogs running. Although poly or nylon is usually used for training, Iditarod rules specify that mushers must use cable-core gang line or cable tie-out lines for each dog. Although it is stronger and can't be chewed through, the newer Kevlar® cable-core gang lines are expensive and prone to kinking. They also become heavy due to their ability to absorb moisture.

© Jeff Schultz/Alaskastock

Each dog wears a padded harness. Tugs lines attach the harnesses to the gang line, which pulls the sled.

HARNESS

Each dog wears a flat nylon collar with a large ring over which a cross-backed harness is slipped. Made of lightweight, padded, one-inch-wide nylon-webbed material, the harness fits around the dog's shoulders and forelegs. It is designed to place the weight on the dog's shoulders and chest, helping to transfer the dog's pulling power to the sled. The harness is attached to the end of the tug line by a heavy snap or carabiner placed on a metal ring or reinforced rope loop.

The first harnesses, made of leather, were similar to horse collars. Today, harness styles are constantly improved to make the dogs' work easier.

NECK LINE

Line that connects a dog's collar to gang line and between the two collars of a double lead. The neck line keeps the dog facing forward and prevents him from straying too far from the rest of the line or from tangling with obstacles. Between 12 and 16 inches long, neck lines are $1/16$- to $1/4$-inch diameter rope, intended to be breakable in case of an emergency.

RACING SLED

A lightweight vehicle that is pulled by the dogs and is the musher's method of transportation across the snow. The frame sits on the runners.

Racing sleds were traditionally built of wood, but new designs may have titanium metal frames.

RIGGING LINE

Collection of lines to which dogs are attached. Includes gang line, tug lines, and neck lines.

RUNNERS

The two bottom pieces of the sled that come in contact with the snow. They extend back of the basket for the driver to stand on. Runner bottoms are usually wood, covered with plastic or Teflon®. This plastic or Teflon® is usually replaced at least once during the race.

SLATS

Thin strips of wood that make up the bottom of a wooden sled basket.

SLED

The most common sleds used in competition today are the basket sled *(photo, pg. 110),* which has a gap between the runners and the sled bag, and the racing toboggan *(photo, pg. 103)* in which the bag rests directly on the runners. Racing toboggans have nearly replaced the smaller and less sturdy basket-type sled. Comprised of a single piece of plastic, the toboggan extends from the handlebar to the brush bar and is bolted directly to the tops of the runners. This creates a lower center of gravity, making the sled less likely to tip over.

The toboggan's runners are shorter than those of the basket sled, but its basket and sled bag are larger, making both sleds the same length, about 8 feet. The toboggan can carry more gear, and is helpful in inclement weather, as it can be turned over to create a shelter. It usually weighs between 25 and 45 pounds. A recent addition to the racing sled is the bicycle seat. Small and lightweight, it allows the musher a slightly more comfortable ride.

Together, the runners and the stanchions help make up the skeleton of the sled. The runners prevent the sled from sinking into the snow. Extending up to 2 feet behind the basket, they create a place for the musher to stand. Most runners now have foot pads with a non-skid surface, or 1-2 feet of synthetic plastic with treads. The stanchions are vertical pieces of wood which rise up from the runners and form the framework of the sled. There are usually one to three stanchions per sled. They are usually bolted to the runners at intersecting points, or the runners and the stanchions are lashed together with nylon cord or babiche.

The handlebar is the highest point on a sled, and looks like an inverted letter "U." As the dogs follow voice commands to turn, the musher controls the sled by twisting the handlebar and shifting his or her weight from side to side. The handlebar is usually wrapped with raw-hide, nylon, tape, hockey tape, or halibut fishing line for added grip and strength. The handlebar also is called the drive bow, the driving bow, the steering bow, and the handle bow. Handlebars also help keep tired drivers from falling off of their sleds. Sometimes mushers tie themselves to the handlebar, and it is not uncommon for a lead dog to arrive at a checkpoint with its musher doubled over the handlebar asleep.

The brake looks like a steel claw, and is attached to a long brace running down the center of the sled. The

© Jeff Schultz/Alaskastock

This basket-style sled has the sled bag resting on slats above the runners. A toboggan-style sled is on pg. 103.

metal prongs point down between the driver's feet. He steps on it and the sled is slowed by the steel claws dragging through the ice and snow. A long spring lifts the brake out of the way when it is not in use. Most contemporary sleds utilize a bar brake shaped like the letter "U." This brake has no internal prongs, but is affixed directly to the runners. Carbide points assure greater durability. In a way, the brake can be considered a misnomer, as it does not actually stop the sled, but rather signals the dogs to stop running.

The snow hook serves as an anchor for the sled and team. The driver steps on the fishhook-like snowhook, pushing it into the snow to secure the team and keep it from running away when the musher steps off the sled.

At the front of the sled is the brush bow, shaped like an inverted U. Serving as a bumper, the brushbow receives the brunt of impact and damage should a collision arise. As strength is crucial, the brushbow is reinforced by wrapping around it a strip of wet rawhide which is then laced into place. Duct tape and nylon cord serve the same purpose. Heavy plastic brushbows have become more and more common, as they are often broken.

The sled bag, resting directly upon the runners in a toboggan-style sled or on a series of slats in a basket-sled, carries all of the musher's gear and equipment, and is sometimes used to transport sick or tired dogs. Made of heavy canvas or nylon, it is fastened to the basket or the runners with Velcro, buckles, and/or lashing grommets. If it is large enough, a musher can crawl inside to seek shelter from a storm.

SNOW HOOK OR ICE HOOK

Heavy piece of metal attached to sled by line. Working like an anchor, the snow hook is embedded in the snow to hold the team and sled for a short time so the musher may get off the sled.

SNUB LINE

Rope attached to the sled that's used to tie the sled to a tree or other object so the musher can leave the sled without losing the team.

STAKE

Metal or wooden post driven into the ground to which dog is tied in the dog yard.

TETHER LINE

A long chain with shorter pieces of chain extending from it. Used to stake out a team when stakes aren't available.

TOBOGGAN-STYLE SLEDS

Sleds with a sheet of plastic as the bottom for their basket.
See also: SLED

TOGGLES

Small pieces of ivory or wood used by Eskimos to fasten tug lines to harness.

TOW LINE

See: GANG LINE

TUG LINE

Line that connects dog's harness to the gang line. Tug lines are usually $1/4$- to $3/8$-inch in diameter, and branch off from the gang line, connecting to the dog's harness at the base of the tail. They are usually three to four feet long, and attach using toggles or brass snaps. A loose tug line signals to the driver that a particular dog is not doing his fair share of the work, although a clever dog will make it appear that he is working by keeping just enough pressure on the gang line.

© Jeff Schultz/Alaskastock

Zach Steer leaves Takotna, riding on the runners of his sled with the dogs lined out in front.

Places

ANCHORAGE

Population: 254,000

The Iditarod makes a date with Anchorage for the first Saturday of every March, and with it comes a circus for the senses.

Snow-removal equipment operators work through Friday night in a weird change of mission. Instead of plowing the snow away, they dump tons of it onto downtown streets. Temporary fencing is installed along both sides of Fourth Avenue for many blocks, stretching from Cook Inlet toward the Chugach Mountains. On Saturday morning there's barely room for a single file of bodies to pass through the fans stacked along the sidewalks. Coffee and hot chocolate sales are brisk, and youngsters are hawking race programs. It's bright and cold.

Mushers wear numbered bibs over heavy winter clothing. They murmur to their dogs, check gear, pause to greet friends, and pose for photos. The attention of the crowd is focused on the starting line beneath a fancy banner. Every two minutes, a team advances to the line, dogs straining against their handlers, the musher riding the brake. Stopped on the mark, with handlers gripping their harnesses, a few dogs look back as if to ask, "What's the hold-up? Let's go."

The announcer begins the countdown from ten and the musher, who has been assuring the team with touches and encouraging words, pats the leaders once more, then lopes back to the sled. At "three-two-ONE!" the dogs, like unbound springs, lunge forward.

Away they run down a corridor between storefronts and packed sidewalks, amid shouts of encouragement, crystallized breath, and thudding applause of mitted

115

© Jeff Schultz/Alaskastock

Anchorage's Fourth Avenue is packed with people during the start of the Iditarod each March.

hands. Taking long, powerful strides, the dogs seem to fly along the main street of Alaska's biggest city, where half the state's population lives, and where—as in the Iditarod itself—the civilized and the wild have made an uneasy alliance. Running on instinct and desire, they begin the 1,100-mile journey to Nome.

Iditarod Country, *Epicenter Press*

ANVIK

(ANN-*vick*)

Population: 82 • Miles from Shakeluk: 25

Miles from Anchorage: 623 • Miles to Nome: 499

During odd-numbered years, the trail follows the southern route and passes through Anvik, where the first musher to arrive wins $3,500 in cash plus a seven-course gourmet meal prepared by a chef from Anchorage's Regal Alaskan Hotel.

BURL ARCH

Ruby musher Emmitt Peters was the first of thousands of mushers to welcome the sight of the burled arch on Front Street in Nome as the finish line of the third Iditarod Trail Sled Dog Race in 1975. But after twenty-five years of greeting weary mushers and teams, the historic arch broke in pieces when city crews were moving it after the 1999 race to the spot next to city hall where it serves a tourist attraction the rest of the year.

The first arch was carved by "Red Fox" Olson, the Red Lantern Award winner of the second race in 1974. That year the finish line was marked with a sprinkling from a packet of Kool-Aid. When Olson and Joel Kottke crossed the finish line, they each had a paper pie plate stuck on a trail marker. Kottke's said "The" and Olson's said "End."

"It was sort of symbolic of the fact there wasn't much of a finish line," said Nome Mayor Leo Rasmussen.

When the Iditarod Trail Committee decided to replace the arch, word went out across the state. Before long, logger Jim Skogstand contacted the committee

© Jeff Schultz/Alaskastock

The burl arch marks the finish line in Nome.

saying he had a beautiful burled spruce tree on his property in Hope that he would donate.

Bob Kuiper of Alaska Wildwoods in Sterling volunteered to carve a 28-foot section of the log into a new arch in time for the 2000 Iditarod. The new arch has more than 50 burls of all shapes and sizes.

Peninsula Clarion, *Heather A. Resz*

CHECKPOINTS AND DISTANCES

Checkpoints	Distance Between	From Anchorage northern route/southern route	From Nome northern route/southern route
Anchorage to Eagle River	20	20	1092/1102
Eagle River to Wasilla	29	49	1063/1073
Wasilla to Knik	14	63	1049/1059
Knik to Yentna	52	115	997/1007
Yentna to Skwentna	34	149	963/973
Skwentna to Finger Lake	45	194	918/928
Finger Lake to Rainy Pass	30	224	888/898
Rainy Pass to Rohn	48	272	840/850
Rohn to Nikolai	80	352	760/770
Nikolai to McGrath	48	400	712/722
McGrath to Takotna	18	418	694/704
Takotna to Ophir	25	443	669/679
[1]Ophir to Cripple	**60**	**503**	**609**
Cripple to Ruby	**112**	**615**	**497**
Ruby to Galena	**52**	**667**	**445**
Galena to Nulato	**52**	**719**	**393**
Nulato to Kaltag	**42**	**761**	**351**
[2]*Ophir to Iditarod*	*90*	*533*	*589*
Iditarod to Shageluk	*65*	*598*	*524*
Shageluk to Anvik	*25*	*623*	*499*
Anvik to Grayling	*18*	*641*	*481*
Grayling to Eagle Island	*60*	*701*	*421*
Eagle Island to Kaltag	*70*	*771*	*351*
[3]Kaltag to Unalakleet	90	851/861	261
Unalakleet to Shaktoolik	42	893/903	219

Shaktoolik to Koyuk	48	941/951	171
Koyuk to Elim	48	989/999	123
Elim to Golovin	28	1017/1027	95
Golovin to White Mt.	18	1035/1045	77
White Mountain to Safety	55	1090/1100	22
Safety to Nome	22	1112/1122	

[1] **On even years, race takes northern route, Ophir to Kaltag.**
[2] *On odd years, race takes southern route, Ophir to Kaltag.*
[3] Northern and southern routes converge at Kaltag.

CRIPPLE

Population: 0 • Miles from Ophir: 60
Miles from Anchorage: 503 • Miles to Nome: 609

The Cripple checkpoint is merely a tent on the Innoko River near the broken-down remains of what was a small settlement. The temperature ranges from 10 above to 55 degrees below zero.

Jules and Leslie Mead, operators of Teeland's Country Store in Wasilla, hosted this checkpoint from 1978 to 1984 when a small T-shaped cabin was still standing. Their custom was to feed the mushers hearty meals at no charge when they stopped at the cabin.

Cripple is the half-way point of the northern route, and the first musher there receives the GCI Dorothy G. Page Halfway Award of $3,000 in gold nuggets.

DALZELL GORGE

The trail goes from "scary to scarier" as mushers cross Rainy Pass, the highest point on the trail, and head through Dalzell Gorge, says Race Manager Jack Niggemyer. He describes the gorge as "probably the most singularly terrifying thing on the whole race. Or it can be, depending on the weather.

"You're going downhill at the bottom of a narrow canyon, winding back and forth across the creek, so you've got a lot of sidehills and open water. And big holes in the ice. And rocks you can't move. Once you get down to the bottom, where it drains into the Tatina River, and you've got to run across there for a couple of miles, overflow is common. We can go put the trail in,

Alaska Stock photo by Jeff Schultz

The Dalzell Gorge is the most terrifying part of the trail, with sidehills, ice, and overflow.

and two hours later, there's icy slush, and two hours after that, it can be bare ground."

Iditarod Country, *Epicenter Press*

EAGLE ISLAND

Population: 0 • Miles from Grayling: 60
Miles from Anchorage: 701 • Miles to Nome: 421

This checkpoint along the southern route was once home to the Conaster family. Ralph, Helmi, and their son Steve lived in a 12- by 14-foot cabin there the year the race first followed the southern route. Helmi died in 1992, and now Ralph and Steve stay in the family's original cabin when they come to commercial fish in summer.

From Eagle Island, the trail follows the Yukon River to Kaltag, the last of the Athabascan villages, where the northern and southern routes rejoin.

Iditarod Country, *Epicenter Press*

EAGLE RIVER

Population: 29,595
Miles from Anchorage: 20 • Miles to Nome: 1092

Pockets of Iditarod fans station themselves along the "urban" trail between Anchorage and the nearby town of Eagle River. Even drivers on the four-lane Glenn Highway can follow the action from their car windows as northbound mushers edge along the foothills of the Chugach Range.

At Eagle River, the mushers are met by their support crews. Teams are unharnessed and loaded into dog trucks for the drive to Wasilla, thus avoiding open water on the Knik River and the often-snowless Palmer Flats.

Iditarod Country, *Epicenter Press*

ELIM

(EE-*lum*)

Population: 281 • Miles from Koyuk: 48

Miles from Anchorage: 989 • Miles to Nome: 123

On the coast of the Bering Sea, the trail into and out of Elim guides mushers through windswept territory. Local people are poised to watch out for travelers, and if necessary will find lost mushers and get them back on the trail.

Some mushers report seeing ghost lights along the trail in this area, mostly near the old settlements along the coast.

Iditarod Country, *Epicenter Press*

© Jeff Schultz/Alaskastock

In 1977, a forest fire raced through the Bear Creek area, leaving behind the Farewell Burn, where snowfall is low and the trail rough. See: FAREWELL BURN, *page 124.*

FAREWELL BURN

About 20 miles below Rohn, the mushers arrive at the infamous Farewell Burn. In 1977, thousands of acres burned in the Bear Creek fire, and the resulting dead-fall, coupled with low snowfall, makes for a bumpy, sled-shredding ride.

FINGER LAKE

Population: 2 • Miles from Skwentna: 45
Miles from Anchorage: 194 • Miles to Nome: 918
Gene and June Leonard manned the Finger Lake checkpoint from their cabin there when the racers first came through in 1973, and Gene entered the race four times himself, finishing twice.

The checkpoint is now at the Winter Lake Lodge owned by Carl and Kirsten Dixon.

The trail through this area is steep and treacherous, winding through heavy timber and sidehills.Snow up to 10 feet deep is not uncommon
                    Iditarod Country, *Epicenter Press*

FOURTH AVENUE

The main street through downtown Anchorage, Fourth Avenue is the site of the ceremonial start of the race on the first Saturday in March. Snow is trucked in to provide footing for the dogs and sleds, and crowds line the sidewalks as the teams begin the race to Nome.

GALENA

(guh-LEEN-uh)
Population: 529 •Miles from Ruby: 52
Miles from Anchorage: 667 • Miles to Nome: 445

Galena is the hometown of 1974 champion Carl Huntington and Edgar Nollner, the last living participant of the 1925 diphtheria Serum Run. Nollner's granddaughter, Rose Yaeger-Lund, organized the Galena checkpoint for the Iditarod from 1973 to 1990, when she moved to Anchorage.

Iditarod Country, *Epicenter Press*

GOLOVIN

(GOL-uh-vin)
Population: 148 • Miles from Elim: 28
Miles from Anchorage: 1017 • Miles to Nome: 95
As the mushers come into this village, they are nearing the home stretch of the race, with only two additional checkpoints before reaching Nome—White Mountain and Safety.

GRAYLING

Population: 208 • Miles from Anvik: 18
Miles from Anchorage: 641 • Miles to Nome: 481
Grayling is one of the checkpoints on the southern route, followed every other year. Through this area, mushers are traveling along the Yukon River, with the prevailing wind in their faces—a grueling factor some years.

GHOST TOWNS ALONG THE TRAIL

Three ghost towns lie along the Iditarod Trail—Ophir, Cripple, and Iditarod. Each was once a bustling gold mining community that saw its peak in the early part of the 20th century. At Cripple, some $35 million in gold was mined between 1908 and 1925. Ophir was named

in the Bible as the lost country, the location of King Solomon's gold mines. And Iditarod was once home to more than ten thousand people who were tied in some way to gold mining. No buildings remain at Iditarod.

Iditarod Silver, *Epicenter Press*

HIGHEST POINT ON THE IDITAROD TRAIL
Rainy Pass at 3,160 feet.

IDITAROD, checkpoint

(eye-DID-a rod)

Population: 0 • Miles from Ophir: 90

Miles from Anchorage: 533 • Miles to Nome: 589

Rusted out equipment and a little trapping cabin are all that stand where once there was a bustling mining hub of ten thousand people. Between 1908 and 1925, when gold was $20 an ounce, about $35 million in gold was taken from the region.

Now, to mark the halfway point on the southern race, sponsor GCI awards a trophy and $3,000 in gold nuggets to the first musher to arrive.

KALTAG

(KAL-tag)

Population: 234

Miles from Eagle Island on southern route: 70

Miles from Nulato on northern route: 42

Miles from Anchorage: 771 • Miles to Nome: 351

At Kaltag, the southern and northern routes converge, so the mushers pass through the village every year. Kaltag is the last Athabascan Indian village before mushers cross an invisible boundary into Inupiat Eskimo country. From here, the trail leaves the Yukon River and heads into the Nulato Hills through Old Woman Pass to reach the Bering Sea.

Iditarod Country, *Epicenter Press*

KNIK

(kuh-NICK)

Population: 272 • Miles from Wasilla: 14

Miles from Anchorage: 63 • Miles to Nome: 1049

On their way to Knik teams pass a massive log building that houses the Iditarod Trail Committee headquarters and museum. The Mushers Hall of Fame is also in Knik, which is home to many notable mushers.

From Knik, mushers leave the road system as the trail winds through Alaska's Bush country on its way to Nome.

Iditarod Country, *Epicenter Press*

KOYUK

(COY-uck)

Population: 258 • Miles from Shaktoolik: 58

Miles from Anchorage: 941 • Miles to Nome: 171

At the head of Norton Sound, Koyuk is the northernmost checkpoint at just shy of 65 degrees north. From Shaktoolik on their way to Koyuk, mushers cross the frozen sea ice on a trail that's all but invisible during storms. Orange-topped trail markers,surveyor's flagging and spruce trees stuck in the ice guide the racers.

Iditarod Country, *Epicenter Press*

MCGRATH

Population: 466 • Miles from Nikolai: 48

Miles from Anchorage: 400 • Miles to Nome: 712

At the confluence of the Kuskokwim and Takotna rivers, McGrath is not accessible by road, but it's a regional hub with stores, restaurants, a bar or two, and a full-service airport.

Many mushers take their mandatory 24-hour layover here. The first musher to hit town receives the Golden Pace Award—a gold nugget watch from the Alaska Commercial Co.

MOUNTAINS

The highest point on the Iditarod Trail is Rainy Pass, at 3,160 feet. At this point the mushers cross over the Alaska Range, which spans much of the state in a east-west curving arc.

Between Nikolai and Ophir mushers traverse the Kuskokwim Mountains. On the southern route, they are in the Nulato Hills between Anvik and Kaltag, where the southern and northern routes converge. After Kaltag, they cross the Nulato Hills en route to Unalakleet.

NATIONAL HISTORICAL TRAIL STATUS

The late Senator Ernest Gruening first proposed the Iditarod as a national trail. But it wasn't until early 1977 that Senator Mike Gravel introduced a bill designating the Iditarod Trail as the nation's first Historic Trail. President Jimmy Carter signed the National Historical Trail Act, which included the Iditarod Trail, in 1978. Today, the Iditarod is one of several National Historic Trails, among them the Oregon, Mormon, Pioneer, Lewis & Clark, Over Mountain, Victory, Nez Perce, Santa Fe, Trail of Tears, Juan Bautista, and Pony Express trails.

Iditarod Silver, *Epicenter Press*

NIKOLAI

(NICK-o-lye)
Population: 125 • Miles from Rohn: 93
Miles from Anchorage: 352 • Miles to Nome: 760
Nikolai, with its unsurpassed view of the back side of Mount McKinley just a hundred miles to the west, is the first of the predominately Native villages mushers pass through in the race. Most residents are Athabascan

Indians. Nikolai has a restaurant and a lodge, as well as the Community hall which serves as the checkpoint.

Iditarod Country, *Epicenter Press*

NO MAN'S LAND

"No man's land is the trail between Fort Davis Roadhouse and the official finish line in Nome. A musher need not relinquish the trail on demand in this area."

Iditarod Rules, 2001

NOME

Population: 3,576 • Miles from Safety: 22
Miles from Anchorage: 1112

As the leading mushers approach town, Nome comes to life, reawakening the excitement of its riotous gold rush past. Everybody is invited to join the frenzy on Front Street. Spectators line the street, flush with celebratory spirits and biting cold. The burl wood archway marking the finish line is in place. A platform stands ready to host post-race interviews and picture-taking sessions of the champion and the leaders draped in yellow roses. The big moment is televised live statewide.

Nome stays on alert until the last of the mushers appears to pick up the Red Lantern Award. Then a team of "trail sweeps" arrives with garbage bags full of dog booties and other debris they've picked up along the trail. Nome then winds down to await another Iditarod.

Iditarod Country, *Epicenter Press*

NORTHERN ROUTE

Every other year, the race follows the northern route, which diverges from the southern route at Ophir, a ghost town left over from the 1908 discovery of gold nearby. On even-numbered years, the northern route takes the mushers from Ophir through the checkpoints at Cripple, Ruby, Galena, Nulato, and Kaltag, where the northern and southern routes converge.

NULATO

(noo-LA-toh)
Population: 359 • Miles from Galena: 52
Miles from Anchorage: 719 • Miles to Nome: 393
Nulato, founded by a Russian trader in 1838, is an Athabascan village and one of the few Native villages where dog mushing hasn't been abandoned for the convenience of snowmachines.

OPHIR

(OH-fur)

Population: 0 • Miles from Takotna: 38

Miles from Anchorage: 443 • Miles to Nome: 669

A ghost town now, Ophir was founded in 1908 after the discovery of gold nearby. Its name stems from a Biblical reference to the source of King Solomon's gold.

The checkpoint is staffed by Dick and Audra Forsgren of Willow, Alaska, who own a cabin at Ophir.

From Ophir, the race route splits. On even-numbered years, it follows the northern route to Cripple. On odd-numbered years, the trail heads south to Iditarod.

Iditarod Country, *Epicenter Press*

RAINY PASS

Population: 2

Miles from Finger Lake: 30

When mushers leave the Finger Lake checkpoint, they travel uphill for miles to Rainy Pass, where they cross the highest point on the trail at 3,160 feet. The trail in this area is narrow and full of switchbacks.

Once over the summit, the mushers head downhill through Dalzell Gorge, described as "probably the most singularly terrifying thing on the whole race."

The Rainy Pass Lodge serves as the checkpoint, but is at Puntilla Lake, elevation 1,800 feet, 18 miles below the summit.

Iditarod Country, *Epicenter Press*

RIVERS

The Iditarod Trail crosses two major rivers.

Mushers encounter the upper reaches of the frozen Kuskokwim just before the McGrath checkpoint. On odd-

© Jeff Schultz/Alaskastock

Rainy Pass is the highest point on the Iditarod Trail at 3,160 feet and among the most scenic.

numbered years, when the race follows the southern route, the mushers reach the Yukon River at Anvik. From there, the trail turns north and a bit west, and follows the western bank of the Yukon until reaching Kaltag, where the southern and northern routes converge. On even-numbered years, the northern route turns north-northwest at Ophir, and the teams don't reach the Yukon until Ruby. At that checkpoint, they turn west and mush along the northern bank of the Yukon to Kaltag. From Kaltag the trail heads west to Norton Sound.

Smaller rivers and streams are common along the trail. In March, these are frozen, but running water under the ice sometimes overflows, causing treacherous patches of overflow ice.

ROHN

(RONE)

Population: 0 • Miles from Rainy Pass: 48

Miles from Anchorage: 272 • Miles to Nome: 840

The Rohn checkpoint consists of a lone cabin near the confluence of the Kuskokwim River's south fork and the Tatina River. Many people consider it to be the most scenic checkpoint on the trail. A roadhouse once stood there to serve the dog-mushing mail carriers and other travelers on the original Iditarod Trail. That building is gone now and the cabin, built in the 1930s, stands in its place. Many mushers take their mandatory 24-hour layover here.

About 20 miles below Rohn, the mushers arrive at the infamous Farewell Burn. In 1977, thousands of acres burned in the Bear Creek fire, and the resulting dead-fall, coupled with low snowfall, makes for a bumpy, sled-shredding ride.

Iditarod Country, *Epicenter Press*

RUBY

Population: 187 • Miles from Cripple: 112
Miles from Anchorage: 615 • Miles to Nome: 497

The first musher to reach Ruby receives a seven-course gourmet meal prepared by the chef from Anchorage's Regal Alaskan Hotel. And along with the dinner comes a cash prize for the First Musher to the Yukon Award.

Ruby is located along the Yukon River at its junction with the Melozitna River. Founded in 1911 when a minor gold rush occurred, its population boomed to more than a thousand. But since the 1920s, fewer than two hundred people, mostly Athabascans, have lived there year-round.

Iditarod Country, Epicenter Press

SAFETY

Population: 0 • Miles from White Mountain: 55
Miles from Anchorage: 1,090 • Miles to Nome: 22

Mushers follow the shore of Norton Sound to Safety, the final checkpoint before Nome. At Safety, the checkpoint building provides the only light for miles. According to Nome Mayor Leo Rasmussen, the present checkpoint building had a previous life in Nome, where in the late 1930s it was a motion picture theater known as the "Nomerama." A half-century later, it was cut into sections and rebuilt at Safety.

The place was so named because of its natural harbor, known for protecting ships. From Safety, mushers must wear their numbered bibs for the final leg of the journey.

Iditarod Country, Epicenter Press

SHAGELUK

(SHAG-a-luck)
Population: 139 • Miles from Iditarod: 65
Miles from Anchorage: 598 • Miles to Nome: 524

Snug along the banks of the Innoko River, Shageluk is an Athabascan Indian community whose name means "village of the dog people." In winter, men run traplines; in summer, the villagers depend on subsistence fishing. On clear March nights, it can still get down to 20 to 30 below zero. Most Shageluk homes are log cabins; newer frame buildings include the school, the village store, and the "Washeteria," where everybody goes to take showers and do their laundry.

Iditarod Country, *Epicenter Press*

SHAKTOOLIK

(shak-TOO-lick)
Population: 199 • Miles from Unalakleet: 40
Miles from Anchorage: 893 • Miles to Nome: 219

From Shaktoolik, mushers have five more checkpoints before Nome. Villagers there pride themselves on predicting who will get to Nome first—studying the way the dogs and the mushers look as they arrive in the village.

Iditarod Country, *Epicenter Press*

SKWENTNA

(SKWENT-na)
Population: 90 • Miles from Yentna: 34
Miles from Anchorage: 149 • Miles to Nome: 963

This checkpoint is located at the confluence of the Yentna and Skwentna rivers, where Norma and Joe Delia head an army of two dozen local volunteers. Some years, the couple have served meals to more than four hundred people in the space of a few days. The race route follows Joe Delia's trapline route for a ways through this area.

Iditarod Country, *Epicenter Press*

SOUTHERN ROUTE

On odd-numbered years, the race route takes the southern route. From Anchorage to Ophir, the route is the same each year. Then at Ophir it diverges. The southern route passes through Iditarod, Shageluk, Anvik, Grayling, and Eagle Island, then goes on to Kaltag where it converges with the northern route. The northern route is followed on even-numbered years.

TAKOTNA

(ta-COT-na)
Population: 51 • Miles from McGrath: 23
Miles from Anchorage: 418 • Miles to Nome: 694

Above the banks of the Takotna River, this village is an important refueling stop for mushers, thanks to the volunteers and villagers who offer sumptuous meals. Mushers, pilots, and journalists are fed like kings with stacks of hot cakes, breakfast meats, burgers, crab, steak, turkey, and the longtime favorites that are always on the stove—moose stew and chili.

Takotna's new community building is the center of hospitality, and the whole village gets involved organizing and helping with the mushers' supplies as they are shipped in before the race passes through—dog food, stove fuel, straw, pails, disposable dishes, and more.

Iditarod Country, *Epicenter Press*

UNALAKLEET

(YOU-na-la-kleet)

Population: 882 • Miles from Kaltag: 90

Miles from Anchorage: 851 • Miles to Nome: 261

The Gold Coast Award, a trophy and $2,500 in gold, is waiting for the first musher to reach Unalakleet—the largest community between Wasilla and Nome. The village is the first checkpoint along the coast, and sudden storms off the Bering Sea can be brutal. Villagers are sure to offer a warm welcome, though. Kids are let out of school and the entire town turns out to welcome the mushers.

Unalakleet is an Inupiat Eskimo word meaning "where the east wind blows." Drifting snow here can reach the rooftops. This is one of the few checkpoints on the trail where mushers change sleds, exchanging their freighting sleds for lighter-weight racing sleds. It's the last of the soft snow; from here on, the landscape is windblown and hard.

Iditarod Country, *Epicenter Press*

VILLAGES ALONG THE TRAIL

See: CHECKPOINTS AND DISTANCES

WASILLA

(wah-SILL-a)

Population: 4,635 • Miles from Eagle River: 29

Miles from Anchorage: 49 • Miles to Nome: 1063

After the ceremonial start on Anchorage's Fourth Avenue, mushers queue up again for the restart in Wasilla. The official clock starts ticking when they leave the starting line. Traveling along the edge of Knik-Goose Bay

Road, the teams follow a trail frequently used by valley snowmachiners. Locals haul barbecue grills and lawn chairs to the ends of their driveways, forming cheering squads that are so close to the trail they can offer passing mushers a "low five." At these parties, ice chests are used not to chill the beer and soda, but to keep the drinks from freezing.

Iditarod Country, *Epicenter Press*

WHITE MOUNTAIN

Population: 209 • Miles from Golovin: 18
Miles from Anchorage: 1,035 • Miles to Nome: 77

At this checkpoint—with only one more, Safety, before reaching Nome—mushers are required to take an eight-hour layover. Usually, the first musher to White Mountain goes on to win. "They just take off right on the button after they take their eight hours," says race volunteer and lifelong White Mountain resident Howard Lincoln. "They don't even wait a minute."

Iditarod Country, *Epicenter Press*

YENTNA

(YENT-na)
Population: 8 • Miles from Knik: 997
Miles from Anchorage:115 • Miles to Nome: 499

The Yentna Station Roadhouse is located on a switchback of the Yentna River called the Big Bend. It is owned and operated by the Gabryszak family, who also serve as checkpoint volunteers some years for the Knik 200 sled dog race, the Klondike 300 sled dog race, the Klondike 400 snowmachine race, the Iditasport, the Junior Iditarod, and the Iron Dog.

For the Iditarod, Jean Gabryzack and her helpers offer free spaghetti dinners to the mushers in exchange for their autographs on posters that go to the volunteers.

Iditarod Country, *Epicenter Press*

Resources

BOOKS

For great reading about the Iditarod and sled dog racing, look for these books from Epicenter Press (www.EpicenterPress.com):

Adventures of the Iditarod Air Force: True Stories about the Pilots Who Fly for Alaska's Famous Sled Dog Race, by Ted Mattson

Father of the Iditarod: The Joe Redington Story, by Lew Freedman

Honest Dogs, A Story of Triumph & Regret from the World's Toughest Sled Dog Race, by Brian O'Donoghue

Iditarod Classics: Tales of the Trail Told by the Men and Women Who Race Across Alaska, by Lew Freedman

Iditarod Country: Exploring the Route of The Last Great Race®, by Tricia Brown

Iditarod Dreams: A Year in the Life of Alaskan Sled Dog Racer DeeDee Jonrowe, by Lew Freedman

Iditarod Silver, text by Lew Freedman, photography by Jeff Schultz (out of print)

Jon Van Zyle's Iditarod Memories: 25 Years of Poster Art from the Last Great Race, by Jona Van Zyle

Lessons My Sled Dog Taught Me: Humor and Heart-warming Tails from Alaska's Mushers by Tricia Brown

Riding the Wild Side of Denali: Alaska Adventures with Horses and Huskies, by Miki & Julie Collins

Spirit of the Wind: The Story of George Attla, Alaska's Legendary Sled Dog Sprint Champ, by Lew Freedman

Other books about sled dog racing and the Iditarod include:

Adventure in Alaska, by S.A. Kramer, Karen Meyer (Illustrator), Random House

Back of the Pack; Don Bowers, Publication Consultants

Fan's Guide to the Iditarod, by Mary H. Hood, et al., Alpine Publications

Iditarod, by Shelley Gill, et al., Algonquin Books

Iditarod: The Great Race to Nome, by Bill Sherwonit, et al, Alaska Northwest Publishing Company

Iditarod: Women on the Trail, by Nicki J. Nielsen, Wolfdog Publications

The Joy of Running Sled Dogs, by Noel K. Flanders, Alpine Publications

The Last Great Race, by Tim Jones, Stackpole Books

Race Across Alaska, by Libby Riddles, Tim Jones, Stackpole Books

The Race to Nome, by Kenneth A. Ungermann, Press North America/Nulbay Associates, Inc.

Running North, by Ann Mariah Cook, Wheeler Publishers

Sled Dog Trails, by Mary Shields, Pyrola Publications

Sled Dogs: Speeding Through Snow (Dogs Helping People), Alice B. McGinty, Rosen Publishing Group

The Speed Mushing Manual, by Jim Welch, Sirius Publishing

Susan Butcher, Sled Dog Racer (The Achievers), by Ginger Wadsworth, Lerner Publication Company

Susan Butcher and the Iditarod Trail, by Ellen M. Dolan, Walker and Co. Library

Winterdance, by Gary Paulsen, Harcourt Brace

The World of Sled Dogs, by Lorna Coppinger, Howell Book House.

Yukon Alone, by John Balzar, et al., Henry Holt & Co.

ORGANIZATIONS

Alaska Dog Musher's Association
PO Box 662
Fairbanks, AK 99707

Alaska Sled Dog and Racing Association
PO Box 110569
Anchorage, AK 99511

Alaska Skijoring and Pulking Association
PO Box 82516
Fairbanks, AK 99708

Copper Basin 300
PO Box 110
Glennallen, AK 99588

Iditarod Trail Committee
PO Box 870800
Wasilla, AK 99687
(907) 376-5155
www.iditarod.com
Iditarod@iditarod.com

International Sled Dog Racing Association, Inc.
(ISDRA)
22702 Rebel Road
Merrifield, MN 56465-4164

Kuskokwim 300
PO Box 300
Bethel, AK 99559

Mushing Magazine
PO Box 149
Ester, AK 99725

Nenana Dog Musher's Association
c/o PO Box 281
Nenana, AK 99760

P.R.I.D.E. (Proving Responsible Information on a
    Dog's Environment)
PO Box 84519
Fairbanks, AK 99708

Yukon Quest International, Ltd.
PO Box 75015
Fairbanks, AK 99707

POSTERS

Official Iditarod Artist Jon Van Zyle, one of Alaska's most popular artists, first created a poster to commemorate the race in 1977; the 2001 poster marked the twenty-fifth anniversary of these official Iditarod posters. Each year, a portion of the profits from Van Zyle's work has supported the Iditarod, with proceeds totaling hundreds of thousands of dollars.

Jon is married to Jona Van Zyle, herself a musher, writer, artist, and freelance museum curator.

Van Zyle's posters and prints may be ordered by visiting the Epicenter Press website:
www.EpicenterPress.com.

P.R.I.D.E.

Acronym for the organization, Proving Responsible Information on a Dog's Environment (PO Box 84519, Fairbanks, AK 99708). Each musher's entry fee in the Iditarod includes membership dues for P.R.I.D.E. and the Iditarod.

WEBSITES

Any internet search engine will find dozens of websites relating to the Iditarod Trail Sled Dog Race, dog mushing, Alaska, sprint racing, and other related topics. Here are a few to get your online Iditarod enjoyment started:

Alaska Magazine: www.alaskamagazine.com

Alaska Public Radio Network:
    www.alaskaone.com/iditarod
Alaska Stock Images: www.AlaskaStock.com
Alaskan Sled Dog and Racing Association:
    www.corecom.net
Anchorage Convention & Visitors Bureau:
    www.anchorage.net
Anchorage Daily News: www.adn.com
Cabela's: www.cabelas.com
Epicenter Press: www.EpicenterPress.com
Fairbanks Daily News-Miner: www.news-miner.com
The (Wasilla, Alaska) Frontiersman:
    www.frontiersman.com
Iditarod Trail Committee: www.iditarod.com
International Sled Dog Racing Association:
    www.isdra.org/
Jeff Schultz Photography: www.Schultzphoto.com
Mushing magazine: www.mushing.com
Nome Convention & Visitors Bureau:
    www.alaska.net/~nome/
Nome Nugget: www.nomenugget.com
Working Dog Web:
    www.workingdogweb.com/Iditarod.htm
Yukon Quest: www.yukonquest.org

YUKON QUEST

The Yukon Quest International Sled Dog Race is Alaska's other long-distance sled dog race. Begun in 1984, the Quest runs between Fairbanks, Alaska, and Whitehorse, Yukon, Canada, along routes traditionally used for mail delivery, trapping, and prospecting.

The 1,000-mile race begins on the second Saturday

in February, alternating the start between Fairbanks and Whitehorse. Mushers finish the race in ten to fourteen days.

The Yukon Quest bills itself as "The Toughest Sled Dog Race on Earth." Checkpoints are farther apart than those of the Iditarod Trail, and, because the race is run in February, temperatures may be colder, varying from 76 degrees below zero to 32 above (Fahrenheit).

The Yukon Quest trail crosses some of the most sparsely populated and undeveloped country in North America. Hard-packed snow, rough gravel, frozen rivers, icy open water, mountainous terrain, or river flats can make the trail fast at times or slow it to a crawl.

For more information on the Yukon Quest, contact Yukon Quest International Sled Dog Race, Fairbanks, AK, (907) 452-7954 or (867) 668-4711.

Final Facts

APPENDIX I
RACE POLICIES - 2001

IDITAROD TRAIL INTERNATIONAL SLED DOG RACE
OFFICIAL 2001 POLICY
PRE-RACE PROCEDURE

1. Entries: Entries will be accepted from June 24, 2000, until December 1, 2000, by the Iditarod Trail Committee (ITC), P.O. Box 870800, Wasilla, Alaska 99687-0800. Kennels entering must indicate the musher's name with their entry. Entries may be presented to the ITC in person by the musher, by proxy or by mail. Entries received in any fashion on June 24, 2000, will draw in the first group. All other entries will draw in the second group.

Mushers who enter in person will sign a log indicating the date and time that they arrived at ITC Headquarters which shall be utilized in determining the order of sign up. A musher will maintain his or her place in the sign up order so long as he or she does not leave ITC property. A musher who has someone log in and remain on the property for him or her, yet arrives for the actual sign up himself or herself, shall be considered to have entered by proxy and not in person. Mushers entering in person shall be followed by mail recording.

Mailed entries will be recorded by postmark. Entries received with the same postmark will be recorded alphabetically for southern route races and in reverse alphabetical order for northern route races.

Entrants by proxy (hand carried but not by the musher) will be recorded in order of appearance after all mushers appearing in person and mail entrants are recorded.

An entry will not be considered valid until the entry fee is paid in full, the race application is completed, signed and turned in, the participant's release is signed, notarized and turned in, and the Nome housing form is completed and turned in. The local contact form and the dog care agreement will be turned in no later than food drop.

The ITC reserves the right to reject entries not in conformance with these policies and rules or from mushers who do not exemplify the spirit and principle of the Iditarod Trail Committee as set forth in the rules, policy, bylaws and mission statement. The decision to reject any entry will be made by the executive committee. A musher may appeal such a decision to the full Board of Directors within fourteen (14) days. The decision of the full Board will be final and binding.

2. Entry Fee. The entry fee is $1,750.00 US, which includes Iditarod and P.R.I.D.E. membership dues, payable on or after June 24, 2000. This entry fee must be received by the ITC or postmarked by midnight, December 1, 2000. Payment of the $1,750.00 US constitutes the musher's intention to enter the race and acknowledges that the musher agrees to comply with these policies and rules.

Upon written request, mushers withdrawing from the race prior to February 14, 2001, may recover $1,500.00 refund from the entry fee. After February 14, 2001, no part of the entry fee will be refunded.

Entry fees received that are not in compliance with this policy shall be refunded and the musher shall not be allowed to participate.

3. Substitutes: There will be no substitute drivers unless approved by the race marshal in case of medical emergency.

4. Musher Qualifications: Mushers must be 18 years of age as of the starting date of the race. For the '01 race, since July 1, 1998, a rookie musher (one who has not completed a previous Iditarod) must have completed two approved qualifying races with an accumulated total of at least 500 miles or must have completed one race of at least 800 miles within the last five racing seasons and a 300-mile race in either the current or previous racing season. A musher must complete any qualifying race and finish in the top 75% of the field or in an elapsed time of no more than 200% more than the elapsed time of the race winner. The performance requirement applies only to races run after July 1, 2000. Written proof of completing this requirement must be submitted to the ITC prior to February 16. Rookie mushers are subject to review before a qualifying board. Rookie mushers will be notified of acceptance or rejection under this rule within (30) days of application. Rookies completing their qualifying race or races after entering must notify the ITC prior to February 14, 2001 to confirm their entry. Rookie mushers must attend the entire rookie musher meeting to be held at 9:00 A.M., Saturday December 9, 2000, and Sunday, December 10, 2000.

5. Purse. The Board and staff shall commit an honest effort to ensure that the $550,000 purse is paid. It shall be paid out as follows:

1st Place	$62,857
2nd Place	55,000
3rd Place	47,143
4th Place	39,286
5th Place	35,619
6th Place	32,476
7th Place	29,857
8th Place	27,238
9th Place	24,619
10th Place	22,000
11th Place	19,381
12th Place	17,286
13th Place	14,667
14th Place	13,619
15th Place	13,095
16th Place	12,571
17th Place	12,048
18th Place	11,262

19th Place 10,738
20th Place 9,952
21th Place 8,381
22th Place 7,333
23th Place 6,286
24th Place 4,190
25th Place 3,667
26th Place 2,619
27th Place 2,095
28th Place 1,833
29th Place 1,571
30th Place 1,310

In addition, the net of the moneys generated through the Idita-Rider program shall be distributed evenly to mushers finishing from 31st place through the Red Lantern winner, up to $1,049 each.

In the event that it is determined by the ITC that it can prudently pay out prize money in excess of $550,000, it may elect to do so. A goal for the ITC is to pay $600,000 for the 2001 race. In the event that it does elect to do so, the amount allocated to each of the top thirty places will be determined by the same percentages as the above breakdown.

6. Shipping of Food and Gear: A musher must comply with shipping directions provided by the ITC. Each container must be clearly marked with name and destination and must weigh no more than 70 pounds. No boxes of any kind may be used as the primary container. No straw, charcoal, fuel or other combustible material may be shipped through the ITC food drops. No cookers, plastic buckets, coolers or dog dishes may be shipped except with any sled that is shipped. Used items must be removed from checkpoints with dropped sleds only.

The musher is advised that food delivered to ITC should be frozen hard. ITC will make every reasonable effort to keep it frozen until picked up by the musher.

All mandatory food must be sent through Iditarod food drops. Additional food and gear not described above may be shipped prior to the start but must be shipped through the checker. Gear damaged beyond repair may be replaced if approved by officials.

Shipping of food and gear must be paid for before the mushers meeting.

Iditarod will ship straw for the teams. Straw can be delivered by the mushers through the mail to supplement the Iditarod program at checkpoints where mail is delivered.

7. Shipping Amounts: An adequate amount of food is required to be shipped to the following checkpoints (minimum of 60 pounds combined weight of food and gear):

Skwentna	Iditarod	Shaktoolik
Rainy Pass	Shageluk	Koyuk
Rohn	Anvik	Elim
Nikolai	Grayling	White Mountain
McGrath	Eagle Island	Nome
Takotna	Kaltag	
Ophir	Unalakleet	

Food and/or gear will not be shipped to the checkpoints of Yentna, Finger Lake or Golovin.

The Safety checkpoint is optional for shipment of gear and/or food.

8. Pre-Race Veterinary Exam: Veterinary paperwork, including pre-race exam forms (one for each dog), proof of vaccination, Dog Microchip Identification Sheet, Verification of Deworming Form and the Veterinarian Signature Form (the letter from the chief veterinarian addressing the veterinarian who performs the physical exams which must be signed along with each Pre-Race Exam Form), has to be delivered to ITC Headquarters by the deadline of 5:00 P.M. on Wednesday, February 28. Non compliance will result in a fine of $100. All examinations must be done on or after February 16, 2001.

A musher must have the team examined at the official pre-race veterinary examination or by an ITC approved veterinarian.

A musher is permitted to have a maximum of 24 dogs screened (microchips, EKG's and bloodwork) in preparation for Iditarod 2001. (All 24 dogs must screened at the original appointment date. There will be no additional screening after that time.) From these, a musher may select a maximum of 20 dogs for listing on the Dog Microchip Identification Sheet, which must be submitted to ITC Headquarters by the previously stated deadline of 5:00 p.m. on Wednesday, February 28. To be listed on the Microchip Identification Sheet, dogs must have had pre-race screening by Iditarod personnel, including a documented microchip implant number, an EKG (EKG) recording and bloodwork. In addition, each must have had a pre-race physical exam to be eligible to race. The musher must select his/her dogs for the start and re-start from those 20 dogs. The maximum number of dogs permitted at the start will be determined by the Race Marshal. A maximum of 16 dogs may be selected for the restart. Once a dog has run in a team, that dog cannot be switched to another team. All dogs entered in the race must have current distemper, parvo, corona and rabies vaccines. Proof of these vaccinations, except for rabies, must come from a veterinarian or a certified lay vaccinator or if administered by the musher, records must include type of vaccine, proof or purchase (i.e., receipt), and date of vaccination in writing. The distemper/parvo/corona vaccine must have been given between April 1, 2000, and February 17, 2001.

Proof of rabies vaccine must come from a licensed veterinarian or certified lay vaccinator. Rabies vaccines must be given no later than February 17, 2001 and must be current through April 1, 2001 according to Alaska State regulations.

All teams must be de-wormed for Echinoccocus Multilocularis with a medication approved by the ITC on or after February 21, 2001.

Mushers will be notified of time and location of pre-race medical evaluation by January 1, 2001. The chief veterinarian will have the authority to remove any dog from competition if, after consultation with a veterinary cardiologist or internist (when available), it is the professional opinion of the chief veterinarian that the dog has an abnormality which may predispose it to a significant risk of injury or death.

The following conditions will prohibit a dog from participating: seizures (epilepsy), syncope (fainting) and/or pregnancy.

For those mushers who have volunteered, ITC will be allowed to draw blood and use non-invasive methods to gather data from dropped dogs and dogs that have completed the race, in the effort to gather information to improve dog care.

9. Jurisdiction and Care: Dogs are under the jurisdiction and care of the chief veterinarian and the veterinary staff from the time they enter the staging area at the start until 72 hours after the team finishes in Nome or scratches, is withdrawn, is disqualified or is released by the veterinary staff.

10. Expired Dog: No dog death is acceptable, but there are some that may be considered unpreventable.

The expired dog must be in the sled bag and covered when the musher arrives at a checkpoint. The musher is to inform a race judge of the expired dog as soon as he/she has checked in.

An expired dog report must be filled out by the musher as soon as he/she reaches the checkpoint.

The musher and/or his/her representative has the option to be present during the trail evaluation and necropsy.

A musher will remain at the initial reporting checkpoint for up to, but no longer than, eight hours to commence the investigation. This period is not to be used as a penalty. A musher will also make him/herself available at all future checkpoints to assist in the investigation. The race marshal or his/her appointed judges may release a musher before the eight hours have expired if the judge is satisfied that the musher is no longer needed to further the investigation.

Dog deaths resulting in disqualification are:

• Signs of cruel, inhumane or abusive treatment
• Cause of death is heat stress, hyperthermia.

A musher will be disqualified if he/she had been advised in writing by a race veterinarian or judge to drop the dog at a previous checkpoint, but opted not to do so, unless the cause of death is clearly unrelated to this written recommendation.

The musher will not be penalized and may continue the race if:

• Cause of death can not be determined
• The cause of death is due to a circumstance, nature of trail, or force beyond the control of the musher. This recognizes the inherent risks of wilderness travel.
• Cause of death is from some unpreventable or previously undiagnosed medical condition.

All dog deaths will be treated as a priority, with every effort being made to determine the cause of death in a thorough and reliable manner.

It is the policy of the ITC to report a dog death to the public in a timely fashion. The ITC will accomplish this by:

• The race marshal shall immediately issue a press release to members of the media identifying the dog's death
• Immediately following the final decision, the race marshal will notify the musher of the decision and will issue a press release containing the findings and the circumstances of the death.

11. Dog Description: Only northern dog breeds suitable for arctic travel will be permitted to enter the race. "Northern breeds" will be determined by race officials.

12. Dog Tags: All dogs leaving the starting line will be electronically marked and tagged. Electronic markers will be installed by ITC personnel unless other arrangements are approved by ITC. Only current tags are permitted. Dogs must be listed by name and tag number/letter and electronic ID on the "team list" provided by the ITC.

13. Dropped Dogs: Mushers may drop dogs at designated dog drops. Dogs dropped at checkpoints may be moved to the closest dog collection area at Anchorage, McGrath, Galena, Unalakleet, or Nome. Dogs may be shipped from the collections' area to a location designated by the musher at the musher's expense.

Dogs dropped in Anchorage, Eagle River, and Wasilla are the musher's responsibility.

Golovin and Nome are not dog drops.

Dogs dropped in all other checkpoints will be transported by the ITC.

A musher is responsible for all of the dogs in the team when at a checkpoint as a race participant and if that musher subsequently scratches, is withdrawn or is disqualified from that checkpoint. If dogs are not moved out of the checkpoint twenty four (24) hours after the musher's departure, dogs can be moved by a commercial carrier at the musher's expense.

Dropped dogs left unclaimed at Eagle River Correctional Center after four days after their arrival will incur boarding charges at the current rate.

14. Food and Gear at Checkpoints: Dog food and supplies must remain at the checkpoint storage area until such time as the musher is officially checked in. Dog food left behind and dog food from scratched, withdrawn and disqualified mushers becomes the property of the ITC and may be used at the discretion of race officials.

15. Advertising, Public Relations & Publicity: The

Iditarod Trail Committee has the unqualified and unrestricted authority to authorize the photographing and collecting of information about the race and all participants therein, and to use such photographs and information for its use in advertising, public relations or other publicity purposes. Each musher shall sign any and all documents as may be requested by the Iditarod Trail Committee. These documents must be executed at the mushers' meeting.

16. Rookie Meeting, Mushers' Meeting and Drawing: Rookie mushers must attend the entire two-day rookie musher meeting to be held on Saturday, December 9, 2000, beginning at 9:00 a.m. and Sunday, December 10, 2000, also beginning at 9:00 a.m. All mushers must attend the entire mushers meeting beginning at 9:00 a.m. on Thursday, March 1, 2001. A fine of from $50 to $500 will be assessed for tardiness or nonattendance at either of these meetings.

The drawing for starting position will be done at the mushers' meeting on Thursday, March 1, 2001. Each musher will draw for his/her starting position. The drawing for positions will be divided. All mushers paying entry fee on June 24 will draw for the first starting positions. The remaining mushers entered will draw for the remaining starting positions.

The musher must be present at the banquet on March 1 where the announcement of the draw order will be made.

17. Race Start and Restart:

a) The official starting date and time for the 2001 race will be March 3, 2001, at 10:00 a.m. in Anchorage, Alaska.

b) The restart will be on Sunday March 4, 2001, at 10:00 a.m. in Wasilla. Teams will leave the restart line on Sunday in the same order and time differential as they left Anchorage on Saturday.

c) The race will be held as scheduled regardless of weather conditions. The starting place and/or restarting place may be changed by the race marshal due to weather and/or trail conditions. A handler may be required at the start and/or re-start at the discretion of the race marshal.

18. Race Timing: For elapsed time purposes, the race will be a common start event. Each musher's total elapsed time will be calculated using 10:00 a.m., Sunday March 4, 2001, as the starting time. Teams will leave the restart at staggered intervals and the time differential will be adjusted during the twenty-four (24) hour mandatory layover. No time will be kept between Anchorage and Eagle River.

Any musher who cannot leave the starting line and/or restarting line in the order drawn must start two (2) minutes after the musher who drew last place has left. Succeeding late start teams will leave in succeeding order at two (2) minute intervals. Every fifth team will leave after three (3) minutes. Time differential for late starters will be calculated according to their scheduled starting time other than the actual starting time.

19. Competitiveness: The race marshal shall have the authority to withdraw a team that is out of the competition and is no longer making a valid effort to compete. The race marshal also has the authority to withdraw a musher whose conduct, in the race marshal's sole and exclusive judgment, constitutes an unreasonable risk of harm to either himself or other persons.

20. Media: Interviews and/or videographic opportunities shall be granted to credentialed members of the media at the discretion of the individual musher prior to, during, and following the race, utilizing the following as specific guidelines:

1.   Only the broadcast rights holder shall be granted live interviews and/or videographic opportunities from two hours prior to the start of the race and until one hour has elapsed following arrival in Nome.

2.   In the event that more than one camera crew is

present in any checkpoint, the first opportunity for an interview shall be granted to the rights holder

3.   No special arrangements for the carrying of the broadcasting and/or recording equipment of any sort may be made by any musher without the express written approval of the Executive Director.

4.   A musher will use his/her best personal effort to insure that the spirit of these guidelines is adhered to. Alleged violation(s) will be reported to the ITC Board of Directors. Flagrant or knowing violations of these guidelines shall be subject to penalties assessed by the ITC Board of Directors including, but not limited to, disqualification and the potential forfeiture of his or her entire purse winnings.

21. Awards Presentation: All mushers who have crossed the finish line up to two (2) hours before the awards presentation must be present and the winner must have his/her lead dog(s) present for recognition. Any musher crossing the finish line who is able to attend the awards presentation ceremony prior to its beginning will be included in the awards presentation ceremony in the proper order. All mushers reaching the banquet before its conclusion will be introduced and given the opportunity to appear before the audience.

OFFICIALS AND PENALTIES

22. Race Officials: The race marshal and judges are responsible for the enforcement of all ITC policies and race rules. Race officials shall consult with the chief veterinarian on all matters relating to dog care and treatment.

23. Protests: A musher may protest any action of a competitor that he/she feels is contrary to the intent of these rules. To be recognized as a legitimate protest, any infraction observed by a musher must be presented in writing at the next checkpoint and in no case more than twenty-four (24) hours after a musher finishes the race.

24. Penalties: Policy and rule infractions may result in issuance of warnings, monetary penalties, time penalties, censure or disqualification. Warnings may be issued by any official. Monetary penalties, censures and time penalties require a majority decision of a three-member panel of race officials appointed by the race marshal. Disqualifications require a unanimous decision of a three-member panel of race officials appointed by the race marshal. The chief veterinarian will be consulted in all cases involving cruel or inhumane treatment.

a) Warnings: Written warnings may be issued for first time or minor violations.

b) Monetary penalties may be imposed up to $1,000 per violation. Such penalties may be deducted from prize money. A musher with unpaid fines may not enter future Iditarod races until such fines are paid.

c) Censure: The Board of Directors, following completion of the race, may censure a musher. A censure may include a warning, either public or private and may eliminate the musher from future races. A written warning, monetary penalty or disqualification must have occurred before censure.

d) Time Penalties: Time penalties may be imposed up to a maximum of two (2) hours per infraction and will be added to the twenty-four (24) hour layover, the eight hour layover on the Yukon River or the eight (8) hour layover at White Mountain. Time penalties will not be levied past White Mountain.

e) Withdrawal: Withdrawal is a process that may be imposed by a three-judge panel, either by a majority or unanimous vote, and which has the effect of involuntarily eliminating the musher and team from the race but which does not imply any deliberate misconduct or violation. The team and musher must leave the trail and may be assisted by the ITC at the discretion of the race marshal.

f) Disqualifications: Mushers shall be disqualified for

rule infractions involving physical abuse of a dog, or for cheating or deliberate rule infractions that give a musher an unfair advantage over another musher. Mushers may also be disqualified for other acts involving cruel and inhumane treatment. It is intended that the nearest involved officials be included on the panel. The musher will be given the opportunity to present his case to each member of the panel prior to the decision.

g) Disqualified and withdrawn teams must leave the trail or forfeit the right to enter future Iditarods.

25. Appeals: Mushers may appeal race official decisions. Appeals pertaining to warnings or monetary fines must be presented in writing to the ITC within ten (10) days following the awards banquet. Appeals pertaining to censure must be presented in writing to the ITC within ten (10) days after receipt of the censure by the musher. Appeals pertaining to withdrawals, disqualifications or time penalties must be presented in writing to ITC within 10 days following the awards banquet. Appeals will be considered at an informal hearing before an appeals board appointed by the president of ITC which will be held within forty-five (45) days of filing the appeal. Review by the appeals board is the exclusive, final and binding remedy for any dispute regarding application of the rules by race officials to a musher and that the decision of the appeals board is non-reviewable either in state or federal courts.

The ITC shall appoint a rules committee immediately after the 2001 race. The rules committee shall be mandated to complete the rules and policy by sign-up date.

APPENDIX II
RACE RULES - 2001

Iditarod Trail Committee Incorporated
PO Box 870800
Wasilla, Alaska 99687-0800
Ph. 907-376-5155 Fax 907-373-6998

The Iditarod Trail International Sled Dog Race shall be an open class race for all dog mushers meeting the entry qualifications as set forth by the Board of Directors of the Iditarod Trail Committee, Inc. Recognizing the varying degrees of experience, monetary support, and residence locations of a musher, the Trail Committee shall encourage and maintain the philosophy that the race be constructed to permit all qualified mushers who wish to enter and complete the race to do so. The object of the race is to determine which musher and dogs can cover the race in the shortest time under their own power and without aid of others. That is determined by the nose of the first dog to cross the finish line. To that end, the Iditarod Trail Committee has established the following rules and policies to govern the race.

1. Checkpoints: A musher must personally sign in at each checkpoint before continuing, except at the Wasilla restart.

2. Mandatory Stops: A musher must personally sign in and out to start and complete all mandatory stops.

Twenty Four-Hour Stop: A musher must take one mandatory twenty-four (24) hour stop during the race. The twenty-four (24) hour stop may be taken at the musher's option at a time most beneficial to the dogs. The checker must be notified by the musher that he/she is taking his/her twenty-four (24) hour stop. Time begins upon notification. The starting differential will be adjusted during each team's twenty-four (24) hour stop. It is the musher's responsibility to remain for the entire twenty-four (24) hour period plus starting differential. The ITC will give each musher the required time information prior to leaving the starting line.

Eight Hour Mandatory Stops: In addition to the mandatory twenty-four (24) hour stop, a musher must take one eight (8) hour stop on the Yukon and one eight (8) hour stop at White Mountain.

None of the three (3) mandatory stops may be combined.

3. Bib: A musher is required to carry his/her official ITC bib from White Mountain checkpoint to Safety checkpoint. The musher must wear the bib in a visible fashion from Safety Checkpoint to Nome. The winner shall continue to wear the bib through the lead dog ceremony. All promotional material, except the bib, must be returned to the ITC at the finish line, or in the case of mushers who scratch, to the checker accepting the musher's scratch form.

4. Sled: A musher has a choice of sled subject to the requirement that some type of sled or toboggan must be drawn. The sled or toboggan must be capable of hauling any injured or fatigued dogs under cover, plus equipment and food. Braking devices must be constructed to fit between the runners and not to extend beyond the tails of the runners. No more than two (2) sleds can be shipped beyond Wasilla. These sleds may be used at the musher's discretion. Sleds or mushers may not be assisted with sails or wheels. Ski poles are allowed. No other sled changes are permitted except that a sled damaged beyond repair may be replaced if approved by an official. Once a sled has been left behind, it cannot be transported along the trail. It cannot be used again unless approved by the race marshal as a replacement for a broken sled.

5. Mandatory Items:

A musher must have with him/her at all times the following items:

1. Proper cold weather sleeping bag weighing a minimum of 5 lbs.

2. Ax, head to weigh a minimum of 1-3/4 lbs., handle to be at least 22" long.

3. One pair of snowshoes with bindings, each snowshoe to be at least 252 square inches in size.

4. Any promotional material provided by the ITC.

5. Eight booties for each dog in the sled or in use.

6. One operational cooker and pot capable of boiling at least three (3) gallons of water.

7. Veterinarian notebook, to be presented to the veterinarian at each checkpoint.

Gear may be checked at all checkpoints except Eagle River, Wasilla, Knik and Safety.

Mushers' diaries will be checked only by the veterinarian.

A $500 fine will be accessed if promotional material is not turned in.

6. Dog Maximums and Minimums: The maximum number of dogs a musher may start the race with is sixteen (16) dogs. A musher must have at least twelve (12) dogs on the line to start the race. At least five (5) dogs must be on the tow line at the finish line. No dogs may be added to a team after the restart of the race. All dogs must be either on the tow line or hauled in the sled and cannot be led behind the sled or allowed to run loose.

7. Unmanageable Teams: A musher may seek the aid of others to control an unmanageable team.

8. Driverless Team: A team and driver must complete the entire race trail including checking in at all required locations. A driverless team or loose dog may be stopped and secured by anyone. The driver may recover his/her team either on foot, with assistance from another musher or mechanized vehicle and continue the race. If a dog team is picked up during an emergency, it is the race marshal's discretion as to whether or not that team must be returned to that point if it is to continue the race. Motorized assistance must be reported to an official at the next checkpoint. If mechanized help is used, the team or dog must be returned to the point where it was lost before the team or dog may continue.

9. Scratched Mushers: A musher scratching from the race is responsible for the transportation of his/her dogs and gear off the trail.

10. Hauling Dogs: A musher may haul dogs in the sled at his/her discretion, however, the musher may not allow any of the dogs to be hauled by another team. Dogs must be hauled in a humane fashion and must be covered if conditions require.

11. Teams Tied Together: Two or more teams may not be tied together except in an emergency. Any team so involved must notify officials at the next checkpoint.

12. Pacing: Pacing is not allowed.

13. Motorized Vehicles: A musher may not be accompanied by or accept assistance from any motorized vehicle that gives help to the musher, including aircraft and snowmachines, except when recovering a loose dog or driverless team.

14. Dog Care: A musher will be penalized if proper care is not maintained. Dogs must be maintained in good condition. All water and food must be ingested voluntarily.

15. Shelter for Dogs: Dogs may not be brought into shelters except for race veterinarians' medical examination or treatment. Dogs must be returned outside as soon as such examination or treatment is completed unless the dog is dropped from the race.

16. Cruel and Inhumane Treatment: There will be no cruel or inhumane treatment of dogs. Cruel or inhumane treatment involves any action or inaction, which causes preventable pain or suffering to a dog.

17. Injured, Fatigued or Sick Dogs: All injured, fatigued or sick dogs that are dropped from the race must be left at a designated dog drop with a completed and signed dropped dog form. Any dropped dog must be left with four (4) pounds of dog food and a reliable chain or cable (16″ to 18″ in length) with swivel snap and collar

18. Expired Dogs: Any dog that expires on the trail must be taken by the musher to a checkpoint. The musher may transport the dog to either the checkpoint just passed, or the upcoming checkpoint. An expired dog report must be completed by the musher and presented to a race official along with the dog. The chief veterinarian will cause a necropsy to be carried out by a board-certified pathologist at the earliest opportunity and shall make every attempt to determine the cause of death. If a board certified pathologist is not available to perform the necropsy within the time frame to preserve the tissues appropriately, (as determined by the race marshal), the gross necropsy and tissue collection will be performed by a trail veterinarian following the guidelines in the Musher and Veterinary Handbook. These tissues will then be examined by a board certified pathologist. The race marshal or his/her appointed judges, will determine whether the musher should continue or be disqualified.

19. Harness and Cables: Dog must leave checkpoints with functional, non-chafing harnesses. A musher must carry cable tie-out lines or have cable in the tow line capable of securing the team. Equipment deemed unsafe by race officials is prohibited.

20. Drug Use: No injectable, oral or topical drug which may suppress the signs of illness or injury may be used on a dog. A musher may not inject any substance into their dogs. No other drugs or other artificial means may be used to drive a dog or cause a dog to perform or attempt to perform beyond its natural ability.

The following drugs are prohibited:

A. Anabolic Steroids

B. Analgesics (prescriptive and non-prescriptive)

C. Anesthetics

D. Antihistamines

E. Anti-inflammatory drugs including but not limited to:
   1. Cortico-steroids (the exception is for use on feet)
   2. Antiprostaglandins
   3. Non-steroidals
   4. Salicylates
   5. DMSO

F. Bronchodilators

G. Central Nervous System Stimulants

H. Cough Suppressants

I. Diuretics

J. Injectable Anticolinergics

K. Muscle Relaxants

L. Tranquilizers & Opiates

Dogs are subject to the collection of urine or blood samples, at the discretion of the testing veterinarian, at any point from the pre-race examination until six (6) hours after the team's finish in Nome. The musher or a designee will remain with the dogs. All results will be sealed and signed for before the tests are considered complete.

A musher must assist the veterinarian in collecting samples whenever requested. If blood or urine testing of a dog reveals any of the prohibitive drugs in the dog, this rule has been violated regardless of when such drugs were administered to the dog.

Mibolerone (Cheque Drops) is permitted only for use as an estrus suppressant in intact females that have not had an ovariohysterectomy. Megesterol acetate (Ovaban) is permitted for use of estrus suppression and medical conditions for which progesterone therapy is appropriate, as approved by the chief veterinarian.

The practice of blood doping, i.e., injection of whole blood, packed blood cells or blood substitutes is prohibited.

Race veterinarians may utilize any of the listed drugs or

other prohibited drugs necessary to maintain a dog's health, however, such dogs will be withdrawn from the race. The use of local or general anesthetics will not be allowed in any form unless the dog is withdrawn from the race.

Personal prescriptions written for and carried by the mushers may not be used on the dogs.

MUSHER CONDUCT

21. Good Samaritan Rule: A musher will not be penalized for aiding another musher in an emergency. Incidents must be explained to race officials at the next checkpoint.

22. Interference: A musher may not tamper with another musher's dogs, food or gear or interfere in any manner with the progress of another team.

23. Food and Gear at Checkpoint: A musher's personal gear, equipment and supplies may not be transported along the trail by mechanized means without the consent of the race marshal.

24. Passing: When one team approaches within fifty (50) feet of another team, the team behind shall have the immediate right of way upon demand. The musher ahead must stop the dogs and hold them to the best of his/her ability for a maximum of one minute or until the other team has passed, whichever occurs first. The passed team must remain behind at least fifteen (15) minutes before demanding the trail.

25. Sportsmanship: Any musher must use civil conduct and act in a sportsmanlike manner throughout the race. Abusive treatment of anyone is prohibited.

26. Parking: A musher must select a campsite off the race trail so that the team cannot interfere with other teams, i.e., no snacking of dogs in the trail. A musher needing to stop momentarily must not interfere with the progress of another team. Teams must be parked at designated localized holding areas in checkpoints in places that do not interfere with the movements of other teams and mushers.

No parking or camping is permitted within one (1) mile of checkpoints or villages.

27. Accommodations: Mushers may only use accommodations at officially authorized locations.

28. **Litter:** No litter of any kind may be left on the trail, in camps, or in checkpoints. All material remaining in checkpoints must be left in designated areas. In localized holding area and on the trail, excessive left over dog food is considered litter. For purposes of these rules, straw is not considered litter.

29. Use of Drugs and Alcohol: Use of illegal drugs as defined by state law or excessive use of alcohol by mushers during the race is prohibited. Iditarod has the right to conduct random drug testing. A musher is subject to collection of urine samples at any point from the start until one (1) hour after each team's finish in Nome.

30. Demand for Food and Shelter: A musher may not make demands for food and shelter along the trail.

31. Outside Assistance: A musher may not receive outside assistance between checkpoints. All care and feeding of dogs will be done only by that team's musher. No planned help, including verbal assistance (i.e. coaching) is allowed throughout the race, at or between checkpoints. All dog maintenance and care of dog teams and gear in checkpoints will be done in the designated localized holding area only. A musher relinquishing the care of his team to leave checkpoint and/or village must withdraw from the race. Penalty for infraction of this rule will be either time penalty or disqualification.

32. Lost Food: A musher may replace lost or unusable dog food shipments at checkpoints through whatever methods are available.

33. No Man's Land: No man's land is the trail between Ft. Davis Roadhouse and the official finish line in Nome. A musher need not relinquish the trail on demand in this area.

34. One Musher per Team: Only one musher will be permitted per team and that musher must complete the entire race.

35. Killing of Game Animals: In the event that an edible big game animal, i.e., moose, caribou, buffalo, is killed in defense of life or property, the musher must gut the animal and report the incident to a race official at the next checkpoint. Following teams must help gut the animal when possible. No teams may pass until the animal has been gutted and the musher killing the animal has proceeded. Any other animal killed in defense of life or property must be reported to a race official, but need not be gutted.

36. ELT or Satellite Tracking Device: While a musher may carry an emergency tracking device, such as an emergency locator transmitter (ELT) or other similar satellite tracking device, activation will make a musher ineligible to continue and will result in withdrawal from the race.

37. Navigation: Mushers are restricted to the use of traditional forms of navigation. This includes time, distance as known or measured on a map, speed as is computed with simple arithmetic and direction as indicated by magnetic compass. Electronic or mechanical devices that measure speed and direction are prohibited, i.e. Loran, night vision goggles and GPS.

THE INTENT OF THESE RULES IS TO ENSURE FAIR COMPETITION AND THE HUMANE CARE OF SLED DOGS. THE RACE SHOULD BE WON OR LOST ON MERIT RATHER THAN TECHNICALITIES. RACE OFFICIALS APPOINTED BY THE ITC ARE RESPONSIBLE FOR INTERPRETING THE RULES IN KEEPING WITH THAT INTENT.

APPENDIX III
IDITAROD FINISHERS, 1973-2000

1973
1. Dick Wilmarth
2. Bobby Vent
3. Dan Seavey
4. George Attla
5. Herbert Nayokpuk
6. Isaac Okleasik
7. Dick Mackey
8. John Komak
9. John Coffin
10. Ron Aldrich
11. Bill Arpino
12. Bud Smyth
13. Ken Chase
14. Ron Oviak
15. Victor Kotongan
16. Robert and Owen Ivan
17. Rod Perry
18. Tom Mercer
19. Terry Miller
20. Howard Farley
21. Bruce Mitchell
22. John Schultz
Scratched:
Dr. Hal Bartko
John Schultheis
Darrel Reynolds
Barry McAlpine
Slim Randles
Raymie Redington
John Luster
Alex Tatum
C. Killigrock
David Olson
Herbert Foster
Ford Reeves and Mike Schrieber

Casey Celusnik

1974
1. Carl Huntington
2. Warner Vent
3. Herbie Nayokpuk
4. Rudy Demoski
5. Dan Seavey
6. Ken Chase
7. Raymie Redington
8. Ron Aldrich
9. Joee Redington, Jr.
10. Dick Mackey
11. Joe Redington, Sr.
12. Tom Mercer
13. Jamie "Bud" Smith
14. Rod Perry
15. Dave Olson
16. Reuben Seetot
17. Robert Ivan
18. Victor Kotongan
19. Terry Adkins
20. Tim White
21. Desi Kamerer
22. Clifton Jackson
23. Mary Shields
24. Lolly Medley
25. Joel Kottke
26. Red Olson
Scratched:
Steve Murphy
Carl Topkok
Richard Korb
John Ace
Bernie Willis
Ward Olanna
John Luster
Don Rosevear

John Coffin
Wilbur Sampson
George Attla
Jack Schultheis
Ralph "Babe" Anderson
Jerry Riley
Bill Vaudrin
Warren Coffin
Tom Johnson
Isaac Okleasik

1975
1. Emmitt Peters
2. Jerry Riley
3. Joee Redington, Jr.
4. Herbert Nayokpuk
5. Joe Redington, Sr.
6. Henry Beatus
7. Dick Mackey
8. Ken Chase
9. Rudy Demoski
10. Eep Anderson
11. Alan Perry
12. Ray Jackson
13. Rick Mackey
14. Victor Kotongan
15. Ralph Lee
16. Robert Schlentner
17. Bill Cotter
18. Chris Camping
19. Bill Vaudrin
20. Darrell Reynolds
21. Richard Burnham
22. Jim Kershner
23. John Ace
24. Mike Sherman
25. Steve Fee
Scratched:

Col. Norman Vaughan
Edward Bosco
Hans Algottsen
Sandy Hamilton
Michael T. Holland
Ginger Burcham
Bobby Vent
Guy Blankenship
Terry McMullin
Lavon Barve
Carl Huntington
Walt Palmer
Charlie Fitka
Doug Bartko
Franklin Paniptchuk
John Komak

1976
1. Jerry Riley
2. Warner Vent
3. Harry Sutherland
4. Jamie "Bud" Smyth
5. Emmitt Peters
6. Ralph Mann
7. William "Sonny" Nelson
8. Dick Mackey
9. Tom Mercer
10. Rick Swenson
11. Joe May
12. Don Honea
13. Alan Perry
14. Ray Jackson
15. Ken Chase
16. Billy Demoski
17. Terry Adkins
18. Rudy Demoski
19. Jack Hooker
20. Ford Reeves
21. Babe Anderson
22. Lavon Barve

23. Jerry Austin
24. Ron Aldrich
25. Richard Burnham
26. Charlie Fitka
27. Steve Jones
28. Clarence Towarak
29. Alex Sheldon
30. William Solomon
31. Allan Marple
32. Peter Nelson
33. Jon Van Zyle
34. Dennis Corrington
Scratched:
Joe Redington, Sr.
Col. Norman Vaughan
Richard Hanks
Trent Long
Bob Schlentner
Peter Kakaruk
John Giannone
Lee Chamberlain
Oran Knox
Mel Fudge
Bruce Mitchell
Phillip Foxie
Steve Fee

1977
1. Rick Swenson
2. Jerry Riley
3. Warner Vent
4. Emmitt Peters
5. Joe Redington, Sr.
6. Dick Mackey
7. Don Honea
8. Robert Schlentner
9. Babe Anderson
10. Jack Hooker
11. Ken Chase
12. Alex Sheldon
13. Pete McManus

14. Terry Adkins
15. Al Crane
16. Howard Albert
17. William "Sonny" Nelson
18. Roger Nordlum
19. Rod Perry
20. Richard Burnham
21. Stein Havard Fjestad
22. Bill Cotter
23. Rick Mackey
24. Sandy Hamilton
25. Bob Chlupach
26. Charlie Harrington
27. Eep Anderson
28. Jim Smarz
29. Duane Halverson
30. Peter Kakaruk
31. Randy DeKuiper
32. Dale Swartzentruber
33. Jerry Mercer
34. Varona Thompson
35. Jim Tofflemire
36. Vasily Zamitkyn
Scratched:
Don Montgomery
Tom Mathias
Ray Jackson
Rudy Demoski
Rick McConnell
Bob Watson
Ron Gould
Franklin Paniptchuk
John Ace
Dinah Knight
John Hancock
William Solomon

1978
1. Dick Mackey
2. Rick Swenson
3. Emmitt Peters
4. Ken Chase
5. Joe Redington, Sr.
6. Eep Anderson
7. Howard Albert
8. Robert Schlentner
9. Jerry Austin
10. Alan Perry
11. Sonny Lindner
12. Ron Aldrich
13. Pete MacManus
14. Bob Chlupach
15. Ron Tucker
16. Terry Adkins
17. Harry Sutherland
18. Richard Burnham
19. Susan Butcher
20. Varona Thompson
21. Joe Garnie
22. Jerry Mercer
23. Charlie Fitka
24. Ernie Baumgartner
25. Jack Goodwin
26. Rick McConnell
27. William Solomon
28. James Brandon
29. Shelley Vandiver
30. John Wood
31. Ray Gordon
32. Gary Campen
33. Col. Norman Vaughan
34. Andrew Foxie
Scratched:
Roger Roberts
Duke Bertke
Mike Demarco
Bill Rose

Babe Anderson

1979
1. Rick Swenson
2. Emmitt Peters
3. Sonny Lindner
4. Jerry Riley
5. Joe May
6. Don Honea
7. Howard Albert
8. Rick Mackey
9. Susan Butcher
10. Joe Redington, Sr.
11. Gary Hokkanen
12. Terry Adkins
13. Dick Peterson
14. Ken Chase
15. Ernie Baumgartner
16. Melvin Adkins
17. Bob Chlupach
18. Victor Kotongan
19. Keith Jones
20. Patty Friend
21. Brian Blandford
22. John Wood
23. Ron Aldrich
24. Eep Anderson
25. Myron Angstman
26. Walter Kaso
27. Jim Rowe
28. Steve Vollertsen
29. Rick McConnell
30. Rome Gilman
31. Bud Smyth
32. Bill Rose
33. Steve Adkins
34. Cliff Sisson
35. Ron Brinker
36. Del Allison
37. John Barron
38. Karl Clausen

39. Jerry Lavoie
40. Gayle Nienhauser
41. Richard Burmeister
42. Jon Van Zyle
43. Jim Lanier
44. Ron Gould
45. Don Montgomery
46. Prentice Harris
47. Gene Leonard
Scratched:
Mark Couch
Isaac Okleasik
Herbie Nayokpuk
Kelly Wages
Terry McMullin
Lee Gardino
Clarence Towarak

1980
1. Joe May
2. Herbie Nayokpuk
3. Ernie Baumgartner
4. Rick Swenson
5. Susan Butcher
6. Roger Nordlum
7. Jerry Austin
8. Walter Kaso
9. Emmitt Peters
10. Donna Gentry
11. Marc Boily
12. Joe Garnie
13. Larry Smith
14. Bruce Johnson
15. Rudy Demoski
16. Dave Olson
17. Dr. Terry Adkins
18. Libby Riddles
19. Harold Ahmasuk
20. Henry Johnson
21. William Bartlett
22. Martin Buser

23. Jack Goodwin
24. DeeDee Jonrowe
25. Ken Chase
26. Bruce Denton
27. Clarence Shockley
28. John Cooper
29. Michael Harrington
30. Marjorie Ann
    Moore
31. Eric Poole
32. Douglas Sherrer
33. Ron Cortte
34. John Gartiez
35. Norman Vaughan
36. Barbara Moore
Scratched:
Bill Boyko
Jan Masek
Ed Craver
Eugene R. Ivey
Larry Cogdill
Robert E. Neidig
John Eckles
Steven R. Conatser
Duke Bertke
Varona Thompson
Fred Jackson
John Barron
Dick Peterson
Lee Gardino
Don Honea, Sr.
Babe Anderson
Don Eckles
Frank Sampson
Warner Vent
Sonny Lindner
Joe Redington, Sr.
Dick Mackey
Alton Walluk
Bruce Woods
Jerry Riley

1981
1. Rick Swenson
2. Sonny Lindner
3. Roger Nordlum
4. Larry Smith
5. Susan Butcher
6. Eep Anderson
7. Herbie Nayokpuk
8. Clarence Towarak
9. Rick Mackey
10. Terry Adkins
11. Duane Halverson
12. Emmitt Peters
13. Jerry Austin
14. Joe Redington, Sr.
15. Harry Sutherland
16. Joe Garnie
17. Gary Attla
18. Donna Gentry
19. Martin Buser
20. Libby Riddles
21. David Monson
22. Bruce Denton
23. John Barron
24. Gene Leonard
25. Bob Martin
26. Neil Eklund
27. Mark Freshwaters
28. Jeff King
29. Steve Flodin
30. Gary Whittemore
31. DeeDee Jonrowe
32. Sue Firmin
33. Mike Storto
34. Dan Zobrist
35. Dennis Boyer
36. Jan Masek
37. Burt Bomhoff
38. Jim Strong
Scratched:
Frank Sampson

Harold Ahmasuk
Robert Ivan
William Webb
Ernie Baumgartner
Gordon Castanza
Douglas Sherrer
Bud Smyth
Ted English
Wes McIntyre
Willie French
Clifton Jackson
Bill Thompson
Jerry Riley
Myron Angstman

1982
1. Rick Swenson
2. Susan Butcher
3. Jerry Austin
4. Emmitt Peters
5. Dave Monson
6. Ernie Baumgartner
7. Bob Chlupach
8. Don Honea, Sr.
9. Stan Zuray
10. Bruce Denton
11. Rick Mackey
12. Herbie Nayokpuk
13. Dean Osmar
14. Terry Adkins
15. Joe May
16. Marc Boily
17. Joe Redington, Sr.
18. Ed Foran
19. Guy Blankenship
20. John Stam
21. Alex Sheldon
22. Mitch Seavey
23. Glenn Findlay
24. John Wood
25. Babe Anderson

26. Jim Strong
27. Ron Cortte
28. Larry Smith
29. Dean Painter
30. Ken Chase
31. Steve Gaber
32. Rose Albert
33. Jan Masek
34. Chris Deverill
35. Leroy Shank
36. Steve Flodin
37. Frank I. Brown
38. Mark "Bigfoot" Rosser
39. Bill Yankee
40. James Cole
41. Richard Burmeister
42. Rick Tarpey
43. Erick Buetow
44. Rome Gilman
45. Jack Studer
46. Ralph Bradley
Scratched:
John Barron
Michael Harrington
Steve Haver
Sue Firmin
Smokey Moff
Bill Rose
Norman Vaughan
Gary Whittemore

1983
1. Rick Mackey
2. Eep Anderson
3. Larry "Cowboy" Smith
4. Herbie Nayokpuk
5. Rick Swenson
6. Lavon Barve
7. Duane Halverson

8. Sonny Lindner
9. Susan Butcher
10. Roger Legaard
11. Joe Runyan
12. Guy Blankenship
13. Dave Monson
14. Sue Firmin
15. DeeDee Jonrowe
16. Howard Albert
17. Bruce Denton
18. Dave Olson
19. Emmitt Peters
20. John Barron
21. Neil Eklund
22. Burt Bomhoff
23. Roxy Woods
24. Walter Kaso
25. Eric Buetow
26. Jim Strong
27. Ken Hamm
28. Vern Halter
29. Shannon Poole
30. William Hayes
31. Walter Williams
32. Christine O'Gar
33. Ted English
34. Bud Smyth
35. Ron Brennan
36. Wes McIntyre
37. Ken Johnson
38. Steve Rieger
39. Connie Frerichs
40. Ray Dronenburg
41. Gary Paulsen
42. Ed Forstner
43. Mark Nordman
44. Dick Barnum
45. David Wolfe
46. Leroy Shank
47. Robert Gould
48. Fritz Kirsch

49. Steve Haver
50. Ron Gould
51. Pam Flowers
52. Norman Vaughan
53. Norm McAlpine
54. Scott Cameron
Scratched:
Terry Adkins
Eugene R. Ivey
Gene Leonard
Beverly Jerue
William Cowart
Alex Sheldon
Bob Bright
Saul Paniptchuk
Ken Chase
Clifton Cadzow
Disqualified:
Les Atherton
Dr. Hal Bartko
Doug Bartko
Jan Masek

1984
1. Dean Osmar
2. Susan Butcher
3. Joe Garnie
4. Marc Boily
5. Jerry Austin
6. Rick Swenson
7. Joe Redington, Sr.
8. Terry Adkins
9. John Cooper
10. Larry Smith
11. Vern Halter
12. Burt Bomhoff
13. Rusty Miller
14. Mark Freshwaters
15. Bob Chlupach
16. Ed Foran
17. Emmitt Peters

177

18. Rick Armstrong
19. Ray Gordon
20. John Barron
21. Jim Strong
22. Bob Toll
23. Eep Anderson
24. Gordon Castanza
25. Ron Cortte
26. Jerry Raychel
27. Diana Dronenburg
28. Sue Firmin
29. Rick Mackey
30. DeeDee Jonrowe
31. Dave Olson
32. Gary Whittemore
33. Eric Buetow
34. Frank Bettine
35. Kari Skogen
36. Calvin Lauwers
37. Dan Cowan
38. Francine Bennis
39. Rick Adkinson
40. Jim Lanier
41. David Scheer
42. Steve Peek
43. Fred Agree
44. Ed Borden
45. Bill Mackey
Scratched:
Ted English
James Cole
Jan Masek
Dave Aisenbrey
Gene Leonard
Ray Dronenburg
Gordon Brinker
Connie Frerichs
Don Honea, Sr.
Lolly Medley
Larry Cogdill
Brian Johnson

Miki Collins
Steve Gaber
William Thompson
Mel Adkins
Bob Sunder
Darrel Reynolds
Vern Cherneski
Ron Brennan
Disqualified:
Guy Blankenship

1985
1. Libby Riddles
2. Duane Halverson
3. John Cooper
4. Rick Swenson
5. Rick Mackey
6. Vern Halter
7. Guy Blankenship
8. Herbert Nayokpuk
9. Sonny Lindner
10. Lavon Barve
11. Tim Moerlein
12. Emmitt Peters
13. Tim Osmar
14. Jerry Austin
15. Terry Adkins
16. Roger Nordlum
17. Glenn Findlay
18. John Barron
19. Raymie Redington
20. Burt Bomhoff
21. Jacques Philip
22. Bob Bright
23. Peter Fromm
24. Steve Flodin
25. Warner Vent
26. Ron Robbins
27. Kazuo Kojima
28. Nathan Underwood
29. Betsy McGuire

30. Kevin Saiki
31. Earl Norris
32. Kevin Fulton
33. John Coble
34. Alan Cheshire
35. Victor Jorge
36. Fred Agree
37. Claire Philip
38. John Ace
39. Rick Armstrong
40. Monique Bene
Scratched:
David Aisenbrey
Terry Hinesly
Susan Butcher
Ted English
Jan Masek
Joe Redington, Sr.
Fred Jackson
Victor Kotongan
Gary Paulsen
Ray Dronenburg
Joseph Maillelle, Sr.
Terry McMullin
Dennis Towarak
Ernie Baumgartner
Rudy Demoski
Norman Vaughan
Armen Khatchikian
Scott Cameron
Chuck Schaeffer
Disqualified:
Bobby Lee
Wes McIntyre

1986
1. Susan Butcher
2. Joe Garnie
3. Rick Swenson
4. Joe Runyan
5. Duane Halverson

6. John Cooper
7. Lavon Barve
8. Jerry Austin
9. Terry Adkins
10. Rune Hesthammer
11. John Barron
12. Guy Blankenship
13. Tim Moerlein
14. Bob Chlupach
15. Jerry Riley
16. Vern Halter
17. Gary Whittemore
18. Ted English
19. Nina Hotvedt
20. Rick Atkinson
21. Rusty Miller
22. Peter Sapin
23. Frank Torres
24. Paul Johnson
25. Martin Buser
26. John Wood
27. Dan MacEachen
28. Jerry Raychel
29. Raymie Redington
30. Mike Pemberton
31. David Olesen
32. Steve Bush
33. Kari Skogen
34. Gordon Brinker
35. Bobby Lee
36. Ron Robbins
37. Dave Scheer
38. Gordy Hubbard
39. Matt Desalernos
40. Alan Cheshire
41. Ray Lang
42. Roger Roberts
43. Allen Miller
44. Armen Khatchikian
45. Don McQuown
46. Mike Lawless

47. Mark Jackson
48. Joe LeFaive
49. Peter Thomann
50. Pat Danly
51. Bill Hall
52. Bill Davidson
53. Scott Cameron
54. Stan Ferguson
55. Mike Peterson
Scratched:
Abel Akpik
John Anderson
Frank Bettine
Roger Bliss
Ron Brennan
Joe Carpenter
Jim Darling
William Cowart
Ray Dronenburg
Don Honea
Fred Jackson
Rick Mackey
Jan Masek
Earl Norris
Joe Redington, Sr.
Douglas Sheldon
John Stam
Norman Vaughan

1987
1. Susan Butcher
2. Rick Swenson
3. Duane Halverson
4. Tim Osmar
5. Jerry Austin
6. Joe Runyan
7. Lavon Barve
8. Ted English
9. John Cooper
10. Martin Buser
11. Joe Garnie

12. Guy Blankenship
13. Jerry Riley
14. Diana Dronenburg
15. Stephen Adkins
16. Matt Desalernos
17. Harry Sutherland
18. Robin Jacobson
19. Bruce Johnson
20. Jacques Philip
21. Sue Firmin
22. DeeDee Jonrowe
23. Terry Adkins
24. Gary Whittemore
25. Herbie Nayokpuk
26. Claire Philip
27. Gary Guy
28. David J. Olesen
29. Dan MacEachen
30. Kazuo Kojima
31. Bruce Barton
32. Dick Mackey
33. Joe Redington, Sr.
34. Dennis J. Lozano
35. John Nels
    Anderson
36. John Coble
37. Michael V. Owens
38. Roger Roberts
39. Pat Danly
40. Bill Chisholm
41. Henry Horner
42. Caleb Slemons
43. Mike Lawless
44. Roy Wade
45. John T. Gourley
46. Don McQuown
47. Matt Ace
48. Brian Johnson
49. Andre Monnier
50. Rhodi Karella

Scratched:
Peter Thomann
Rick Mackey
Raymie Redington
John Barron
Burt Bomhoff
Gordy Hubbard
Libby Riddles
Gordon Brinker
Joe LeFaive
David Aisenbrey
Withdrawn:
Carolyn Muegge
Tony Burch
Norman Vaughan

1988
1. Susan Butcher
2. Rick Swenson
3. Martin Buser
4. Joe Garnie
5. Joe Redington, Sr.
6. Herbie Nayokpuk
7. Rick Mackey
8. Lavon Barve
9. DeeDee Jonrowe
10. Robin Jacobson
11. Jerry Austin
12. Jan Masek
13. Lucy Nordlum
14. Jacques Philip
15. Bill Cotter
16. Tim Osmar
17. Dan MacEachen
18. John Patten
19. Harry Sutherland
20. Matt Desalernos
21. Bill Hall
22. Darwin McLeod
23. Horst Maas
24. Ted English

25. Jerry Raychel
26. John Barron
27. Dewey Halverson
28. Peter Thomann
29. Conrad Saussele
30. Burt Bomhoff
31. Frank Teasley
32. Peryll Kyzer
33. Ken Chase
34. Babe Anderson
35. Ian MacKenzie
36. Mike Tvenge
37. Mark Merrill
38. John Suter
39. John Gourley
40. Jennifer Gourley
41. Peter Kelly
42. Tim Mowry
43. Matt Ace
44. Gordon Brinker
45. Lesley Anne Monk
Scratched:
Tim Moerlein
Terry Adkins
Joe Runyan
Brian Carver
Ray Dronenburg
Norman Vaughan
Disqualified:
Stan Ferguson

1989
1. Joe Runyan
2. Susan Butcher
3. Rick Swenson
4. DeeDee Jonrowe
5. Lavon Barve
6. Martin Buser
7. Guy Blankenship
8. Rick Mackey
9. Joe Redington, Sr.

10. Tim Osmar
11. Jacques Philip
12. Matt Desalernos
13. Bob Chlupach
14. John Barron
15. Joe Garnie
16. Libby Riddles
17. Jerry Riley
18. Bill Cotter
19. Frank Teasley
20. Terry Adkins
21. Richard Self
22. Jerry Austin
23. Mitch Brazin
24. Diana Dronenburg
25. Jamie Nelson
26. Linwood Fiedler
27. Tim Mowry
28. Bill Cavaney
29. Karin Schmidt
30. Bernie Willis
31. Pat Danly
32. Kathy Halverson
33. Kazuo Kojima
34. Frank Winkler
35. Conner Thomas
36. John Suter
37. Duane Lamberts
38. Bob Hoyte
Scratched:
Kevin Saiki
Carolyn Vaughan
Joe LeFaive
Michael Madden
Bill Chisholm
Gary Whittemore
Mike Ross
David Aisenbrey
Norman Vaughan
Roger Roberts
Jan Masek

1990
1. Susan Butcher
2. Joe Runyan
3. Lavon Barve
4. Tim Osmar
5. DeeDee Jonrowe
6. Robin Jacobson
7. Rick Swenson
8. Linwood Fiedler
9. Joe Garnie
10. Martin Buser
11. Bill Cotter
12. Rick Mackey
13. Michael Madden
14. Jacques Philip
15. Sonny Russell
16. John Barron
17. Matt Desalernos
18. John Gourley
19. Jerry Austin
20. Bill Chisholm
21. Dan MacEachen
22. Norm Stoppenbrink
23. Mike Owens
24. Terry Adkins
25. Joe Redington, Sr.
26. Mitch Brazin
27. Kevin Saiki
28. Diana Dronenburg
29. Bob Chlupach
30. Harry Sutherland
31. Don McEwen
32. Raymie Redington
33. Frank Winkler
34. Bill Hall
35. Beverly Masek
36. Malcolm Vance
37. Roy Wade
38. Roy Monk
39. Dave Breuer
40. Duane Lamberts

41. Emmitt Peters
42. Bob Hickel
43. Macgill Adams
44. Lynda Plettner
45. John Suter
46. Larry Harris
47. Greg Tibbetts
48. Bryan Moline
49. Jim Wood
50. Bert Hanson
51. Peter Kelly
52. Pecos Humphries
53. Bill Davidson
54. Lorren Weaver
55. Lars Ekstrand
56. Larry Munoz
57. John Ace
58. Paul Byrd
59. Terry Hinesly
60. Norman Vaughan
61. Steve Haver
Scratched:
Guy Blankenship
Tim Mundy
Chuck Schaeffer
Pascal Nicoud
Mike Ross
Frank Teasley
Leslie Monk
Joe LeFaive
Disqualified:
Jerry Riley

1991
1. Rick Swenson
2. Martin Buser
3. Susan Butcher
4. Tim Osmar
5. Joe Runyan
6. Frank Teasley
7. DeeDee Jonrowe

8. Matt Desalernos
9. Rick Mackey
10. Bill Cotter
11. Kate Persons
12. Jeff King
13. Jacques Philip
14. Jerry Austin
15. Michael Madden
16. Ketil Reitan
17. Lavon Barve
18. Peryll Kyzer
19. Terry Adkins
20. Bill Jack
21. Beverly Masek
22. Laird Barron
23. Joe Garnie
24. Rick Armstrong
25. Linwood Fiedler
26. Burt Bomhoff
27. Dan MacEachen
28. Dave Olesen
29. Raymie Redington
30. Dave Allen
31. Joe Redington, Sr.
32. Jerry Raychel
33. Mark Nordman
34. Malcolm Vance
35. Macgill Adams
36. Nikolai Ettyne
37. Alexander Reznyuk
38. Tony Shoogukwruk
39. Rollin Westrum
40. Brian Stafford
41. John Suter
42. Roger Roberts
43. Larry Munoz
44. Jim Cantor
45. Terry Seaman
46. Kazuo Kojima
47. Rich Bosela
48. Pat Danly

181

49. Dave Breuer
50. Chris Converse
51. Sepp Herrman
52. Lynda Plettner
53. Jon Terhune
54. Gunner Johnson
55. Urtha Lenharr
56. Tom Daily
57. Mark Williams
58. Catherine Mormile
59. Don Mormile
60. Brian O'Donoghue
Scratched:
David Aisenbrey
Nels Anderson
Roy Monk
Gary Moore
John Ace
Sonny Russell
Robin Jacobson
Steve Fossett
Alan Garth
Bill Peele
Barry Lee
Ken Chase
John Barron
Gary Whittemore

1992
1. Martin Buser
2. Susan Butcher
3. Tim Osmar
4. Rick Swenson
5. DeeDee Jonrowe
6. Jeff King
7. Vern Halter
8. Rick Mackey
9. Doug Swingley
10. Ketil Reitan
11. Matt Desalernos
12. Bruce Lee

13. Claire Philip
14. Ed Iten
15. Bill Cotter
16. Kate Persons
17. Lavon Barve
18. John Barron
19. Dan MacEachen
20. Joe Garnie
21. Kathy Swenson
22. Sonny Lindner
23. Beverly Masek
24. Jerry Austin
25. Linwood Fiedler
26. Dave Olesen
27. Bill Jack
28. Frank Teasley
29. Rick Armstrong
30. Terry Adkins
31. Bob Chlupach
32. Burt Bomhoff
33. Bill Hall
34. Gary Whittemore
35. Tomas Israelsson
36. Kathy Tucker
37. Susan Cantor
38. Roy Monk
39. Lynda Plettner
40. Norm Stoppenbrink
41. Joe Redington, Sr.
42. Raymie Redington
43. Charlie Boulding
44. Mike Williams
45. Nels Anderson
46. Kim Teasley
47. Steve Fossett
48. Jon Terhune
49. Bob Holder
50. Jim Oehlschlaeger
51. Cliff Roberson
52. Pete Johnson
53. Steve Christon

54. Skin Wysocki
55. Mellen Shea
56. Bill Bass
57. Bob Hickel
58. Debbie Corral
59. James Reiter
60. Loren Weaver
61. Jim Davis
62. John Peterson
63. Vern Cherneski
Scratched:
Tim Mundy
Catherine Mormile
Carolyn Muegge-
   Vaughan
Norman Vaughan
William Orazietti
Robin Jacobson
Pascal Nicoud
Emmitt Peters
Sonny Russell
Joe Runyan
Eep Anderson
Krista Maciolek
Bob Ernisse

1993
1. Jeff King
2. DeeDee Jonrowe
3. Rick Mackey
4. Susan Butcher
5. Tim Osmar
6. Martin Buser
7. Matt Desalernos
8. Doug Swingley
9. Rick Swenson
10. Bruce Lee
11. Vern Halter
12. Joe Runyan
13. Claire Philip
14. Kathy Swenson

15. John Barron
16. Joe Garnie
17. Linwood Fiedler
18. Sonny Lindner
19. Bill Cotter
20. Kate Persons
21. Dan MacEachen
22. David Olesen
23. Jerry Austin
24. Laird Barron
25. Kathy Tucker
26. Diana Dronenburg
27. Frank Teasley
28. Lynda Plettner
29. Terry Adkins
30. Dewey Halverson
31. Mike Williams
32. Mark Nordman
33. Bob Holder
34. Jason Barron
35. Keizo Funatsu
36. Ketil Reitan
37. Pecos Humphreys
38. Peryll Kyzer
39. Jim Oehlschlaeger
40. Skin Wysocki
41. Jerry Louden
42. Pat Danly
43. Stan Smith
44. Jack Goode
45. Roger Haertel
46. Paul Rupple
47. Joe Carpenter
48. Mark Chapoton
49. Kirsten Bey
50. Bert Hanson
51. Harry Caldwell
52. John Peterson
53. Spencer Thew
54. Lloyd Gilbertson
Finisher:

Beverly Masek
Scratched:
Julius Burgert
Norman Lee
Terry Hinesly
Val Aron
David Aisenbrey
Gary Moore
Robin Jacobson
Rick Townsend
Robert Morgan
Lavon Barve
John Shandelmeier
Disqualified:
Dave Branholm

1994
1. Martin Buser
2. Rick Mackey
3. Jeff King
4. Rick Swenson
5. Bill Cotter
6. Doug Swingley
7. Charlie Boulding
8. Tim Osmar
9. DeeDee Jonrowe
10. Susan Butcher
11. Matt Desalernos
12. Kate Persons
13. Vern Halter
14. Peryll Kyzer
15. Robin Jacobson
16. David Olsesen
17. Ramy Brooks
18. Linwood Fiedler
19. Diana Dronenburg
20. Kenth Fjelborg
21. Ramey Smyth
22. Jerry Austin
23. Ketil Reitan
24. Bruce Lee

25. Laird Barron
26. Frank Teasley
27. Stan Smith
28. Mike Williams
29. Lynda Plettner
30. Bill Hall
31. Bob Holder
32. Gus Guenther
33. Terry Adkins
34. Jack Berry
35. Krista Maciolek
36. Robert Somers
37. Aaron Burmeister
38. Cliff Roberson
39. Simon Kinneen
40. Bob Morgan
41. Steve Adkins
42. Dave Branholm
43. Bob Ernisse
44. Harry P. Caldwell
45. Ron Aldrich
46. Jon Terhune
47. Kazuo Kojima
48. Roger Bliss
49. Bruce Moroney
50. Mark Chapoton
Scratched:
Beth Baker
Lisa M. Moore
Lloyd Gilbertson
Mark Nordman
Jamie Nelson
Chris Converse
Rick Townsend
Withdrawn:
Catherine Mormile

1995
1. Doug Swingley
2. Martin Buser
3. Bill Cotter

183

4. DeeDee Jonrowe
5. Charlie Boulding
6. Rick Mackey
7. Jeff King
8. Vern Halter
9. Tim Osmar
10. Rick Swenson
11. Peryll Kyzer
12. John Barron
13. Linwood Fiedler
14. Matt Desalernos
15. David Sawatzky
16. Ramy Brooks
17. Jerry Austin
18. David Olesen
19. Ramey Smith
20. Mitch Seavey
21. John Gourley
22. Mark Wildermuth
23. David Milne
24. Randy Adkins
25. Harry Caldwell
26. Jack Berry
27. Art Church
28. Cliff Roberson
29. Dave Branholm
30. Robert Salazar
31. Bob Holder
32. Kazuo Kojima
33. Libby Riddles
34. David Dalton
35. Don Lyrek
36. Nicolas Pattaroni
37. Pat Danly
38. Paula Gmerek
39. Rollin Westrum
40. Robert Bundtzen
41. Wayne Curtis
42. Jon Terhune
43. Nikolai Ettyne
44. Kjell Risung

45. Susan Whiton
46. Max Hall
47. Tim Triumph
48. Larry Williams
49. Ben Jacobson
Scratched:
Andy Sterns
Kathleen Swenson
Diana Moroney
Robert Somers
Pecos Humphreys
Barrie Raper
Lorren Weaver
Don Bowers
Keizo Funatsu

1996
1. Jeff King
2. Doug Swingley
3. Martin Buser
4. Tim Osmar
5. DeeDee Jonrowe
6. Bill Cotter
7. Charlie Boulding
8. David Sawatzky
9. Vern Haler
10. Peryll Kyzer
11. Ramy Brooks
12. David Scheer
13. Robin Jacobson
14. Lavon Barve
15. Mitch Seavey
16. John Barron
17. Linwood Fiedler
18. Cim Smyth
19. Roger Dahl
20. Sven Engholm
21. Jerry Austin
22. Johnny Baker
23. Tomas Israelsson
24. Dewey Halverson

25. Bruce Lee
26. Paul Gebhardt
27. Diana Moroney
28. Andy Willis
29. Dave Olesen
30. Nicolas Pattaroni
31. Conner Thomas
32. Steve Adkins
33. Kazuo Kojima
34. Michael Nosko
35. Harry Caldwell
36. Mike Webber
37. Jim Davis
38. Randy Romenesko
39. Susan Whiton
40. Lori Townsend
41. Bill Gallea
42. Mark Nordman
43. Aaron Burmeister
44. Rob Carss
45. Ararad Khatchikian
46. Dave Branholm
47. Lisa Moore
48. Don Bowers
49. Andy Sterns
Scratched:
Bill Hall
Roy Monk
Rich Bosela
Stan Zuray
Jack Berry
Kjell Risung
Mark Black
Withdrawn:
Rick Swenson*
Ralph Ray
Linda Joy
Bob Bright
*Decision to withdraw
Rick Swenson was
reversed by the
Appeals Board.

1997
1. Martin Buser
2. Doug Swingley
3. Jeff King
4. DeeDee Jonrowe
5. Vern Halter
6. Lavon Barve
7. Bill Cotter
8. Ramy Brooks
9. Peryll Kyzer
10. Tim Osmar
11. John Baker
12. Sven Engholm
13. Charlie Boulding
14. Paul Gebhardt
15. Ramey Smyth
16. Mitch Seavey
17. Linwood Fiedler
18. Mike Williams
19. David Sawatzky
20. Kris Swanguarin
21. Nick Pattaroni
22. Michael Nosko
23. Jack Berry
24. Krista Maciolek
25. Raymie Redington
26. Harry Caldwell
27. Robert Bundtzen
28. Jean Lacroix
29. Randy Adkins
30. Keli Mahoney
31. Ross Adam
32. Mark Lindstrom
33. Al Hardman
34. Shawn Sidelinger
35. Dan Seavey
36. Joe Redington Sr.
37. Wayne Curtis
38. Bill Bass
39. Bob Hickel
40. Don Bowers

41. Suzan Amundsen
42. Sonny King
43. Jerome Longo
44. Ken Chase
Scratched:
John Barron
Dave Branholm
Ted English
Bob Ernisse
Max Hall
Linda Joy
Jerry Raychel
James Ritchie
Lori Townsend

1998
1. Jeff King
2. DeeDee Jonrowe
3. Charlie Boulding
4. Mitch Seavey
5. John Baker
6. Ramey Smyth
7. Martin Buser
8. Linwood Fiedler
9. Doug Swingley
10. Vern Halter
11. Rick Swenson
12. John Barron
13. Paul Gebhardt
14. Sven Engholm
15. David Sawatzky
16. Joe Garnie
17. Tim Osmar
18. Ramy Brooks
19. Bill Cotter
20. Mark May
21. Christopher Knott
22. Zack Steer
23. Mike Williams
24. Juan Alcina
25. Sony King

26. Raymie Redington
27. Steve Adkins
28. Harry Caldwell
29. Hans Gatt
30. David Milne
31. Robin Jacobson
32. Ted English
33. Lynda Plettner
34. Shawn Sidelinger
35. Jerome Longo
36. Matt Hayashida
37. Andy Willis
38. Ross Adam
39. James Ritchie
40. Gus Guenther
41. Stephen Carrick
42. Jim Lanier
43. Jeremy Gebauer
44. Sam Maxwell
45. Kimarie Hanson
46. Linda Joy
47. Bill Snodgrass
48. Cindy Gallea
49. Chris Lund
50. Matthew Giblin
51. Brad Pozarnsky
Scratched:
Suzan Amundsen
Rob Carss
Ken Chase
Roy Monk
Maria Hayashida
Kris Swanguarin
Don Bowers
Keli Mahoney
Terry Adkins
Jack Berry
Mike Nosko
Dave Lindquist

1999
1. Doug Swingley
2. Martin Buser
3. Vern Halter
4. Rick Swenson
5. Charlie Boulding
6. Paul Gebhardt
7. Jeff King
8. John Baker
9. Sven Engholm
10. Ed Iten
11. Mitch Seavey
12. Ramey Smyth
13. Linwood Fiedler
14. Bill Cotter
15. Dave Sawatzky
16. Rick Mackey
17. Joe Garnie
18. Tim Osmar
19. Harald Tunheim
20. Christopher Knott
21. Hans Gatt
22. Sonny King
23. Mike Williams
24. Sonny Lindner
25. Juan Alcina
26. Ken Anderson
27. Jerome Longo
28. Robert Bundtzen
29. Peryll Kyzer
30. Mike Nosko
31. Russell Lane
32. Raymie Redingon
33. Matt Hayashida
34. Frank Teasley
35. Shawn Sidelinger
36. Jon Little
37. Max Hall
38. Lynda Plettner
39. Aaron Burmeister
40. Dario Daniels

41. Bill Hall
42. Jim Lanier
43. Jim Gallea
44. Don Bowers
45. Shane Goosen
46. Judy Currier
47. Jeremy Gebauer
Scratched:
Linda Joy
Harry Caldwell
DeeDee Jonrowe
John Barron
Steve Carrick
Steve Crouch
Ted English
Dan Dent
Robert Moore

2000
1. Doug Swingley
2. Paul Gebhardt
3. Jeff King
4. Ramy Brooks
5. Charlie Boulding
6. Rick Mackey
7. Martin Buser
8. Rick Swenson
9. Mitch Seavey
10. Bill Cotter
11. Ramey Smyth
12. Hans Gatt
13. Bruce Lee
14. Zack Steer
15. John Barron
16. Tim Osmar
17. Juan Alcina
18. Sonny King
19. Linwood Fiedler
20. DeeDee Jonrowe
21. Vern Halter
22. John Baker

23. Jon Little
24. Ed Iten
25. Harald Tunheim
26. David Sawatzky
27. Tony Willis
28. Mike Williams
29. Raymie Redington
30. Aaron Burmeister
31. Diana Moroney
32. Joran Freeman
33. Bryan Imus
34. Nils Hahn
35. David Milne
36. Russell Lane
37. Al Hardman
38. James Ritchie
39. Mike Nosko
40. Emmitt Peters
41. Ross Adam
42. Jerome Longo
43. Shawn Sidelinger
44. Jamie Nelson
45. Billy Snodgrass
46. Blake Freking
47. Max Hall
48. John Dixon
49. Roy Monk
50. Steve Adkins
51. Aaron Peck
52. John Bramante
53. Anna Bondarenko
54. Paul Ellering
55. Kevin Kortuem
56. Bob Hempstead
57. Caleb Banse
58. Vickie Talbot
59. E. de la Billiere
60. Dan Govoni
61. Trisha Kolegar
62. Bill McKee
63. Dan Dent

64. Melanie Gould
65. James Wheeler
66. Lynda Plettner
67. Dave Tresino
68. Fedor Konyukhov
Scratched
Jerry Riley

Karen Ramstead
Rob Greger
Bill Bass
Cindy Gallea
Shane Goosen
Mike Murphy
David Straub

Rich Bosela
Nelson Shughart
Harry Caldwell
Ted English
Withdrawn:
Neen Brown

APPENDIX IV
2001 ENTRANTS

Juan Alcina
John Baker
John Barron
Anna Bondarenko
Charlie Boulding
Robert W. Bundtzen
Aaron Burmeister
Ramy Brooks
Martin Buser
Stephen Carrick
Rob Carss
Bob Chlupach
Art Church
Buck Church
Bill Cotter
Devan Currier
Wayne Curtis
Pedro Esteban
    Curuchet
John Dixon
Ted English
Paul Ellering
Nikolai Ettyne
Jann Faust
Linwood Fiedler
Morten Fonseca
Joran Freeman
Cindy Gallea
Hans Gatt
Paul Gebhardt

Shane Goosen
Dan (Guido) Govoni
Ben Gray
Nils Hahn
Max Hall
Jason Halseth
Vern Halter
Gwen Holdmann
Ed Iten
G.B. Jones
DeeDee Jonrowe
Chuck King
Jeff King
Sonny King
Ron Koczaja
Peryll Kyzer
Russell Lane
Jim Lanier
Jon Little
Jerome Longo
Rick Mackey
Lance Mackey
Elizabeth Manning
Mark May
Judy Merritt
Andy Moderow
Roy Monk
Bob Morgan
Bruce Moroney
Mike Nosko

Tim Osmar
Lynda Plettner
Paul Pettyjohn
Karen Ramstead
Ray Redington, Jr.
Raymie Redington
Ryan Redington
Jerry Riley
Wally Robinson
Jessica Royer
Palmer Sagoonick
Dan Seavey
Danny Seavey
Mitch Seavey
Ramey Smyth
Gerald Sousa
David Straub
Michael Suman
Rick Swenson
Doug Swingley
Thomas Tetz
Stacy Tostenson
Dave Tresino
Norma Warner
Clinton Warnke
Mike Williams
Aliy Zirkle

(champions in italics)

187

Index

How You Can Help

Our goal for Iditarod Fact Book is accurancy and completeness. Do you have suggestions for changes, additions or corrections? If so, we'd like to hear from you. Send your comments to:

Epicenter Press
Attention: Iditarod Fact Book
Box 82368
Kenmore, WA 98028

or e-mail us at:

Feedback@EpicenterPress.com.

About the Editor

Sue Mattson lived in Fairbanks, Alaska, for twenty-five years, where she was a reporter, editorial page editor, and managing editor for the *Fairbanks Daily News-Miner.* Originally from Bellevue, Washington, Mattson and her husband, Joel, returned there in 1994. She has edited and designed several other books for Epicenter Press.

About the Researcher

Andrea Bachhuber was an intern at Epicenter Press during the summer of 2000. She will graduate from Whitman College with a bachelor of arts degree in English in spring 2001.

About the Photographer

Jeff Schultz has been the official photographer of the Iditarod Trail Sled Dog Race since 1982. An Alaskan since 1978, Schultz grew up in the San Francisco area where he nurtured a love of the outdoors and photography. At 18 he moved to Alaska and launched his career as an outdoor photographer. He owns and operates Alaska Stock Images, representing more than a hundred photographers. He and his wife, Joan, and their two children, Ben and Hannah, live in Anchorage.

About the Illustrator

Jon Van Zyle is recognized throughout the United States and the world for his striking paintings of Alaska's wildlife and landscapes. More than two hundred of his works have been published as limited edition prints and posters over twenty-some years. Van Zyle and his wife, Jona, live near Eagle River, Alaska. They own a team of Siberian huskies, and Jon has run the Iditarod twice.

More Mushing Books from Epicenter Press

JON VAN ZYLE'S IDITAROD MEMORIES

illustrations by Jon Van Zyle • Stories by
Jona Van Zyle • #887 - Hardbound - $16.95
  This handsome gift book contains colorful reproductions
  of the annual Iditarod posters and stories to go with them.

HONEST DOGS

Brian Patrick O'Donoghue • #778 - Softbound - $16.95
  Enjoy the drama of the race through this punishing
  personal journey.

FATHER OF THE IDITAROD

Lew Freedman • #755 - Softbound - $16.95
An inspirational biography of Joe Redington
Sr., the man who founded the thrilling 1,000-
mile race.

ADVENTURES OF THE IDITAROD AIR FORCE

Ted Mattson
#593- Softbound - $12.95

Colorful and exciting stories of the volunteer
pilots supporting the race.

IDITAROD COUNTRY

Tricia Brown / Photos by Jeff Schultz • #666 - Hardbound - $16.95
  Follow the historic trail that connects Native villages, abandoned gold-mining towns, remote lodges and homesteads.

IDITAROD DREAMS

Lew Freedman & DeeDee Jonrowe • #291 - Softbound - $13.95
  An absorbing account of a year in the life of a musher preparing for the Iditarod.